LIVING A LIFE OF YES

How to Seize Opportunities
and Discover Your Uncommon Life

JAMES & SARAH CAMMILLERI

──── foreword by ────
JOHN C. MAXWELL

New York • Florida

LIVING A LIFE OF YES
How to Seize Opportunities and Discover Your Uncommon Life

Written by James and Sarah Cammilleri
Published by Elevating Christian Ministries

Copyright © 2021
James and Sarah Cammilleri / Elevating Christian Ministries, LLC
All rights reserved | 1st Edition

This is a work of non-fiction. All references to real persons, living or dead, are made by the authors with the expressed consent of the persons mentioned. Where this consent has not been given, names have been changed to protect the rights of those individuals.

No part of this publication may be reproduced, stored in a retrieval system, or transmitted in any form or by any means electronic, mechanical, photocopying, recording, or otherwise without the prior written permission of the publisher and copyright owner.

Unless otherwise noted, all scripture quotations are taken from The Holy Bible, New International Version® NIV®
Copyright © 1973 1978 1984 2011 by Biblica, Inc.™
Used by permission. All rights reserved worldwide.

Edited by Jennifer Sell
Cover Design by Christopher Hopper
Interior Design by Kayla Curry
Cover photo by Kristina Smith
Author photo by Pietro Volpato

ISBN: 9798681767473

Contents

Introduction	ix
1. KILL THE COMMON LIFE	1
Haiti and the Uncommon Life	2
What Keeps People Bound to the Common Life?	4
The Anatomy of a No	6
Everyone's Noes Look Different	8
2. THE CRUCIBLE	15
Where Do Yeses Come From?	17
From the Ashes	19
3. LEANING TOWARD GOD	25
Leaning Like Heaven	27
Getting the Heart Right	29
Moving Forward in Worship	31
4. BUCKLE UP	39
This Car Has More Than One Gear	40
Now What, God?	44
5. IS THIS HAPPENING?	49
When God calls	51
Building a Ministry of Yeses	55
You Want Us to Build a What?	56
The Gift of Partnership	58
Tests and Their Outcomes	61
6. BREAKING FOR HAITI	65
From the Head to the Heart	66
Pay Attention to the Themes of Your Life	70
"I Need Help Feeding Children."	72

7. THERE'S NO SUCH THING AS A BAD YES	75
Lessons Always Come Back Around	77
Getting Out of the Boat	79

8. BUILDING GREATNESS OUT OF YESES	85
The Best Big Things Start Small	87
When God Multiplies Stuff, Look Out	91

9. SECRETS TO GROWING STRONG YESES	95
Lessons in Rice Country	97
The Beauty of Getting Organized	99

10. EMPOWERING OTHERS TO DISCOVER THEIR YESES	103
Investing Without Harming	103
We Bring This, You Bring That	106

11. WHEN YES FEELS TOO HEAVY	113
The Fool's Art of Telling God What to Do	114
When Flesh Gets in the Way	117
Questioning the Call Is a Good Sign	120

12. FOUR TIPS TO STAYING ON TASK	125
1.) Acknowledge Who You Are Working For	125
2.) Be a Person of Principle	127
3.) Look for the Lessons	129
4.) Mentor Up, Reach Out	130

13. TAKING ON THE IMPOSSIBLE	133
When Heaven Gets Behind You	137
Progress Is Progressional	138

14. LIVING ON THE OTHER SIDE OF YES	141
1.) Keep Recording, Keep Talking	142
2.) Value People Above Profits	144
3.) ROI vs. ROI	146
4.) The Power of the Proper People	148
5.) Faith Over Fear	150
6.) Pitch a Wide Tent, Cast a Wide Net	152
Your Future Is Waiting	154

Learn More 157
Endnotes 159

Foreword

My friends, James and Sarah, have written a fantastic book called "Living a Life of Yes."

I'm so happy they want to help you say yes more in your life.

As you say yes and you walk in obedience and through open doors, you will uncover things that you thought you would never discover! I often say that obedience, saying yes, is only understood on the back end. Not on the front end.

I know for myself, when I was seventeen years old, my big yes was when I answered the call to ministry. I was still just a teenager but that yes has opened up thousands and thousands of doors. And yet, I would also say this: the moment I say no, the doors close.

What I've discovered the most about people is that they may say an occasional yes but they don't live a life of yes. If I just say an occasional yes every time another opportunity presents itself and become an unsettled hesitant leader, I will miss out. The world is changed by men and women who say the calling is bigger than me, the mission is bigger than me, and the cause is bigger than me, so the answer is yes!

I have a wonderful friend named Larry Stocksdale who I had cast a vision of transformation to about 5,000 leaders. In the green room after the service, Larry looked at me and said, "John, the answer's yes."

"Good, Larry," I replied. "What do you mean the answer's yes?"

"Well, whatever you need, the answer is yes! I live on the other side of yes." And he meant every word of it. He's had an incredibly successful, significant life.

I love the name of this book because I believe that people who make a difference do so because they are willing to say yes even when they didn't understand why. They were willing *before* they had counted all the costs. They were willing when they didn't know the complete path or know all the answers— just to say yes to a higher calling and to God.

James and Sarah live and breathe a life of yes, and I just adore that about them. They are never on the outside asking, "Should we go in? When should we go in?" They just get in the game.

This is the life of James and Sarah, and I pray that it will be yours too.

John C. Maxwell

John C. Maxwell
July 2020

Introduction

Moving forward is hard work, especially when life's current seems to be working against you.

A broken marriage, a lost child, a surprise pink slip, or a bad prognosis from a doctor are curve balls that can set even the most resilient person back. That's because the business of life-living, like any other business, can be challenging. Depression, anxiety, and fear are relentless, as is the frustration that we aren't doing anything significant with our lives. Sometimes, these feelings are downright paralyzing.

But hardship doesn't mean our lives must be hopeless, nor does it preclude us from living a meaningful life. Learning to recognize difficulty as a necessary foundation is one of the many keys to discovering life's tremendous significance.

Our purpose with this book is to encourage you to take

Introduction

steps of faith, no matter how big or small they seem, and discover the beauty of enjoying the unique journey that God has you on. You may be staring at a mountain that looks insurmountable. Similarly, you may be overwhelmed by the sheer volume of responsibilities you're carrying or the tasks on your ever-growing to-do list. Thinking that you are alone when walking through challenging circumstances can be suffocating. But we are here to tell you that you are not alone and that hope is on the way.

Yes, the work of personal transformation is no joke. Forget overnight self-improvement schemes. Reprogramming our heads and hearts can take years, and it is often painful and expensive. Just ask anyone who has been through a difficult season or experienced a catastrophic loss, and they'll tell you that bouncing back is not as easy as the rubber balls make it look. But that doesn't mean recovery is impossible. We discover permission to succeed when we recover from life's hardest blows.

The Old Testament shows us that pain, failure, and bad decision-making were par for the course. The Bible seems full of stories that display the human ability to mess things up and suffer the consequences, no matter who or what caused them. And yet, out of suffering came tremendous hope. There is, perhaps, no more significant theme in all of the Old Testament than Yahweh rescuing the children of Israel from Pharaoh and bringing them through the desert into the Promised Land.

Journeying toward new lands full of promise is not easy.

Introduction

Such journeys are usually quite challenging. But they're doable. And, more than anything, they're rewarding when done well. Of all things that positively marked the children of Israel, it was their obedience to trust God that ultimately saw them through. It was those steps—the ones marked with faith—that moved them closer to the Promised Land, while the actions undertaken with human effort inevitably pulled them away. The people who led the nation most successfully where those who kept their eyes on the horizon and leaned into the promises of God regardless of their surroundings. They were people who learned to say yes to God and no to worldly distractions.

No matter what obstacles you're facing or dreams you're hoping for, we hope you find encouragement and in our story. We experienced painful setbacks in our previous relationships and businesses. There were moments where God felt distant, and pain was louder than love. And yet we found incredible life in trusting the Holy Spirit and learning to say yes to him even when doing so didn't make sense. Yes, everyone's journey is unique. But as we learn to discern God's heart together, we glean from each other's experiences in the hope of following God more faithfully through difficult seasons. What we present in the chapters that follow are principals that have helped transform our lives, taking us from seasons of darkness and frustration to seasons of light and health. We share them with you in the belief that they will help encourage you in your journey.

Introduction

If there is one underlying theme to what follows, it is learning to say yes to every opportunity God brings your way. Saying yes keeps the propeller spinning while God steers the boat. Saying yes also creates momentum against the adverse currents of life. Additionally, other people tend to want to be around things in motion, which means they'll add their energy to your direction. Saying yes has gravity to it, which not only pulls you toward your destiny but brings other people along in theirs.

As the title suggests, saying yes has become one of the great themes of our lives, to such a degree that we decided to write a book about it. We believe that the power hidden inside this simple concept is enough to transform your life too. Whether you are trying to figure out who you want to be when you grow up—regardless of how many birthdays you've celebrated—or whether you're trying to climb your way out of a terrible mess, learning to recognize and say yes to the opportunities around you will propel you forward like nothing else.

We need no more compelling argument than this: God is saying yes over your life. Right now, in unseen realms, the Lord himself is contending for you. He is the one rooting you on, affirming your significance, and urging you forward. The great New Testament writer Paul stated that the Holy Spirit "intercedes for us through wordless groans" (Romans 8:26), while John wrote that Jesus himself is our advocate (1 John 1:21). Even the Old Testament scriptures forecasted Jesus being the "friend who sticks closer than a brother" (Proverbs 18:24). While it may not feel like it, the fact remains that God is cheering you on, as is all of heaven (Hebrews 12:1).

Saying yes to divine opportunities is, at its core, an act of agreement. It's us getting on the same page as heaven. If God is saying yes over our future, then we ought to be as well—and we should be curb-kicking everything else that's not. In the pages that follow, we'll investigate what saying yes looks like, how to watch out for things that will impede your ability to say yes, and how to strengthen every "yes decision" that you make. Finally, we'll examine what it looks like to live on the other side of yes.

This book includes many stories from our journeys, both as individuals and as a married couple. As a result, you'll sometimes find us referring to ourselves in the third person, or taking ownership of individual sections in order to personalize the storytelling. This is not a slip-up by our editor but highly intentional. Not only do the various perspectives draw readers into our lives, but they highlight another guiding principle that we will discuss later—that of being faithful to recount the miracles God has done for us. Since faith comes by hearing (Romans 10:17), we believe that part of what will help you gain traction by saying yes in your life is hearing about how we said yes in ours.

We are excited to give you a glimpse into what God has done in us and through us. Some of it may astound you—all of it amazes us. Much of the richness of our relationships, financial success, and ministry favor might seem like we're boasting. That's because we are, especially since we know who's

Introduction

behind it all. Unfortunately, many of the meanings behind the Bible's promises regarding prosperity were marred by and for North American Christians in the last century. This is unfortunate, both because "prosperity Gospel" teaching is so damaging and because it robbed the church and her members of seeing God's heart for earthly provision.

Instead, when we see that God wants to make us "most prosperous in all the work of your hands" (Deuteronomy 30:9), and charges us to be diligent so that "everyone may see your progress" (1 Timothy 4:15), boasting does not highlight our accomplishments but God's faithfulness (1 Corinthians 1:31).

But no matter what you may think of our business or ministry success, it is imperative to us that you understand we are ordinary people living extraordinary lives. We hail from western New York State and grew up in unexceptional circumstances. At first glance, you might not think there is anything of note about our lives. But as we pull back the curtain on our journey, showing you where we came from and explaining what God is doing, we hope you arrive at the same conclusion we have: we serve a creative, generous, and joyful God who loves being present for his kids.

The rest of what follows is not for the faint of heart. Learning to say yes and to live an uncommon life of extraordinary significance requires passion, energy, and tenacity. It is also costly. Far more expensive, however, is a life devoid of saying yes. And if you read the previous words "passion, energy, and tenacity" and thought "I'm running on empty as it is," then we believe you're holding the right book to refuel and refocus.

Whether you're reading this because someone thought you could use it or because you found the title inspiring, we want you to know that your best days are ahead. God knows you have incredible significance, and we agree with him.

We invite you to discover the power of saying yes.

ONE

Kill the Common Life

I, James, used to joke with my employees that one day I'd end up in Tahiti, surrounded by gorgeous women, aquamarine waters, and enough fine dining to make kings jealous.

And then God put me in Haiti.

The most amazing part is that being in the worst parts of Haiti has made me so happy. And if I had to live in Tahiti, I'd probably be miserable—unless I was doing similar work to what we're doing in Haiti.

To those seeking fame and fortune for self-gratification, going from Tahiti to Haiti and finding happiness doesn't add up. To them, I went from images of bikini-clad women fanning me to being covered in sweat-caked filth. And I understand their dismay. The latter is as far from the former as the mythical "American dream" is from Christians in countries where they will never earn more than two dollars per day.

If current James were to show up and tell young James about what was to come, young James would have blown him off. Young James was out to make himself rich. But what young James didn't know was that while he was working hard to say yes to all his internal desires, he was simultaneously saying no to invitations to things much more gratifying than anything else he was chasing. That's because there's usually a mountain of difference between what we want and what we need.

Haiti and the Uncommon Life

Haiti is a land of strange dichotomies. Lush hillsides plunge to crystal clear waters, while the smells of burnt plastic and smoldering garbage sting the inside of your nose. Smiling children wave and dance in ramshackle huts, dressed in their only articles of clothing and going days or even weeks without a meal.

Horns honk at all hours of the day as vehicles jockey for the right of way. Forget pedestrian crossings or common courtesy—this is survival of the fittest. And the bigger your truck, the more people move out of your way.

The land is hot, dusty, and filled with the smell of sewage. The average visitor will take multiple showers to get the smell off their skin. And whatever you imagine about corruption in the local government, it's worse.

So why would a successful couple from western New York

who owns and operates sixty restaurants be so in love with such a seemingly destitute environment? Arguably, nothing is enticing about the Haitian landscape to someone preoccupied with the creature comforts afforded by first-world living. What is alluring, however, is that Haiti, to us, represents the pinnacle of what it means to be unstuck.

We are convinced that it is impossible to go a day without meeting someone who feels stuck in their first-world life. (Let the irony of that statement sink in for a moment). We hold the world's collective knowledge on a device in the palm of our hand, and yet, according to the Gallup 2019 Global Emotions Report, people are "sadder, angrier and more fearful than ever before"[1]. Whether they are dealing with frustrations at home with a spouse, at work with a dead-end job, or in what we fill the rest of our days with—which often amounts to binge-watching streamed shows or staring at our mobile phones—many people feel stuck in life. The feeling is like waking up, looking in the mirror, and not recognizing the person who's looking back. Even if things seem to be going all right, we still find ourselves asking, "How did I get here?" It's as if the train of life picked up speed, forgot to let us off at the right stop, and then suddenly broke down in the middle of nowhere.

What we just described is what we consider the common life. It is the path followed by those who have not chosen to explore what lies beyond the boundaries of normal life. It can also be the route of others, who, although they decided to venture into the unknown at one time, eventually returned to a mundane life marked by complacency and apathy. Such decisions do not make a person bad; sometimes, we're simply tired from the blows we have endured in the boxing ring of life. But decisions to remain in the common realm do speak to the manner that we are handling God's greatest gift to us outside of himself—the gift to live life to its fullest.

Regardless of whether or not people's reasons for remaining stuck are legitimate, we argue that such a common life does not need to be commonplace. In fact, scripture is quite clear about Jesus wanting to give us an uncommon experience, one marked by abundance (John 10:10). This means that no matter where we live, who our family and friends are, how much money we make, or what natural abilities we have, every Christian has the unique potential to live a very uncommon life.

What Keeps People Bound to the Common Life?

We don't believe for a second that people want to remain broke, destitute, friendless, or without purpose. And anyone who claims that they want to is faking. The reality is that all people crave a place to belong and a work to get behind. In short, we desire to be significant. This is a part of how God has wired us. But so often, what holds people back from a life of significance is something they don't even know that they're doing.

They're saying no.

When we first share this secret with people, many of them look at us like we are crazy. "James and Sarah, what do you mean, saying no? I feel like saying yes has gotten me into my mess as it is." But after we take time to share our story and explain what the power of saying yes is really about, their eyes begin to widen as understanding dawns on them.

First of all, the "saying yes" that many people are referring to usually has to do with committing to things that God never asked them to do. They are "me yeses," not "God yeses." We'll discuss this in-depth later on. For now, however, it's essential to recognize that not all yeses are equal and that many things we think we're saying yes to are actually "noes" in disguise.

Perhaps the single most significant no in disguise is saying yes in order to perpetuate the status quo. Preserving normal is a powerful motivator, and it must not be underestimated. The energy it takes to correct an unhealthy marriage is arguably greater than the energy it takes to grit our teeth and bare it. Indeed, such an assertion does not take into account the emotional toll such silence may take on us. Still, it serves to underpin the idea that keeping things "as they are" is far more enticing to us as people than paying the price to embrace sweeping change.

This is the same reason many people never take the necessary steps to change career paths. The idea of using up valuable savings, attending more schooling, or undertaking a relocation is enough to keep anyone in their dead-end job. And then there's the fear of confronting a boss or telling a spouse. This doesn't imply we should startle anyone with drastic choices, but it serves to illustrate the many obstacles to making a career change.

Wherever change is concerned, the easiest thing is to stay put and say no to the new, the interesting, or the fortuitous. Saying no keeps everything normal. Opportunities are, inherently, the enemy of the status quo because they offer something different than the life we're currently living. The worst part about saying no, however, is that the more often we say it, the easier it becomes. Eventually, we can reach a place where we're living a life of no to the point that we're not only oblivious to new opportunities but resistant to them. This is a dangerous place, resulting in the modification of the saying, "He or she wouldn't know a good opportunity if it jumped up and hit them in the face."

The Anatomy of a No

Opportunities to say yes to God's heart for us are far more prevalent than we might guess. Sometimes we think God gives "one-shot deals." If we miss it, it's gone for good. And while that may be true of unique opportunities, it does not mean that God does not continue to present opportunities to us in general. But problems arise when we condition ourselves to say no as a knee-jerk reaction. As a result, we not only miss the first opportunity, but we create a habit of missing all subsequent opportunities. Noes have a pesky way of interfering with the paths of our lives and reflect deeper issues on why we feel so overwhelmed.

So what do noes look like, and where do they come from?

Some of our strongest noes are connected to fear. Fear of

the unknown can be extremely debilitating and cripple even the best of us. For such individuals, all of life's worst possible scenarios play out in our minds until we can't seem to get ourselves to move at all. Where once we saw an opportunity, suddenly we see a bottomless pit. Instead of leaning forward into life, we end up retreating.

If coworkers invite us out for dinner, we retreat into our non-social cave because of the embarrassment we suffered the last time someone invited us out. Little did we know that God had an important meeting waiting for us that would have opened an impossible door.

If a family member invites us on a road trip or a unique voyage overseas, we find ourselves petrified to get on the plane or commit to the unknown destination city, all because we have allowed fear to sabotage our potential.

Other times, even for the seemingly affluent among us, fear takes the form of comfort. It becomes easier to remain where we are than to brave the boundaries that lead to the unknown. But such "fear in disguise" is as sad as it is paralyzing. If we are not careful, we will miss our most significant opportunities because comfort is cheaper than courage.

Still, other times the fear of not having enough leads us to say no to opportunities that, while they seem out of reach, God was setting up for us. Our mistake, instead, was one that failed to exercise faith—to leap into the unknown. Perhaps one of the most important things to realize is that real wealth has almost nothing to do with monetary affluence, but affluence of the heart. The wealthiest people we know are those who not only have learned how to grow wealthy but who first learned how to be benevolent, to take risks with what little they had, and to fight the urge to say no when God was inviting them to step out in faith.

So, what is the enemy of the change we so desperately desire in our lives? It's saying no, whether passively or actively, to the new challenges and unexplored horizons that get offered to us. If you feel stuck today, and the idea of living an uncommon life despite being an ordinary person feels far away to you, begin by going back to the last "no" you remember giving to a promising opportunity. This is not an exercise meant to stir guilt or regret, but it is intended to help identify the key motivators that cause you to choose the status quo instead of the new opportunity.

Everyone's Noes Look Different

Just as we mentioned that not all yeses look the alike, the same is true about noes. While one person's no may be resistance to needed therapy, and another person's no is a refusal to move across the country, our noes were different from one another but just as detrimental.

For me, Sarah, my common life began in a rural farming town in western upstate New York. (Yes, upstate New York is more than just "whatever's north of New York City" and can be broken up into lots of different regions). I was raised in the church, but after graduation I stopped attending. My life consisted of whatever everyone else was doing and several failed attempts to find that elusive life of significance that people claimed to be pursuing.

Instead, I was working at a Burger King in my hometown at the age of fifteen. It was a good job, and I was good at it. But I had this growing feeling in my gut that I was meant for more—to be and do more. That said, I must express that serving food is not a negative thing. If anything, I'm serving more food today than ever before. And much of our business success is *because* of Burger King. Helping people by providing food is one of the noblest and most edifying jobs anyone could have the privilege of doing.

My purpose in mentioning that I was not leading the life of significance that I wanted is to say that I had not connected my passion for people with my capacity to meet human needs. Instead, I was going through my day, clocking in and out, and doing my best to be significant in the ways that I knew how. Even though I had gone to college to pursue a degree and was financially independent, I still sensed that my life was ordinary. For all intents and purposes, I felt stuck.

I didn't know it at the time, but I was saying yes in small ways that would eventually lead to bigger and bigger yeses.

FOR ME, James, my common life looked very different than Sarah's. In fact, to most people, it looked like I had it all.

I discovered at thirteen years old that I had a knack for the restaurant business, like my father and grandfather before me.

Beyond just bussing tables, I realized I could make money offering to do all the waitresses' extra work at my uncle's restaurant. They paid me to do their clean up, and I'd stay late Friday night only to return at 4:00 a.m. Saturday to wash dishes. My skills and dedication grew so much that by age sixteen, my uncle gave me charge over particular days. From menu selection to food prep to execution and clean up, the restaurant was mine, and I exponentially increased my uncle's profitability. People loved the food too. So much so that by the time I was seventeen, I had started my own catering business.

But when I got to college, I left the restaurant business behind. Or so I thought. My dream of becoming a fighter pilot ended when I learned just how long I'd need to commit to being in the military, so I returned home to help my father run a new Burger King that he'd acquired. As I'd done with my uncle's restaurant before, I took my dad's store that was doing $500,000 per year in a town of 8,000 people to over $1.2 million per year in twenty-four months. Not long after, I purchased three stores of my own, knowing I could make a lot of money.

But it wasn't enough.

My background—my "norm"—was full-service dining. So I kept a notebook of restaurant ideas for a year and then used my profits to invest in opening my own restaurants. The Mundo Grill served world cuisine; Table 7 served wood-fired pizzas and doubled as a downtown Rochester nightclub; Mangia grilled up classic Italian dishes; and Duo was an opulent high-end dining experience. Everything I touched turned to gold. As a result, young James was cocky and self-absorbed. He was strategic, pragmatic, full of high-energy, and he drove fancy cars and lived in an elegant house with a beautiful wife and two children. He had it all.

But that all changed in 2007.

It's safe to say that every person has at least one "oh crap" moment in their life. Mine was a restaurant investment turned nightmare. Due to several factors, both those in and out of my control, I ended up losing over $1 million in three months. At my fine-dining restaurant, I was barely breaking even with a weekly payroll of $8,000. For those unfamiliar with running a business, if you're only making payroll, that is, paying your employees, you're not paying for anything else, like food costs, gas, electricity, cleaning, plowing, insurance, and maintenance (to name a few).

As a result, I was forced to liquidate assets, downsize my family's home, and look for ways to get cash fast. My marriage at the time took a turn for the worst when disagreements broke out over what we were willing to sell and what was non-negotiable. Eventually, things got so bad that the relationship could no longer support what we'd come to expect of it, nor our lifestyle.

As strange as it may sound, this moment of failure was the end of my common life. I recognize that most people don't run multiple restaurants at once. But for the family I grew up in, this was relatively normal. An important thing to realize is that what is common for you is not necessarily what is common for others. It's not how much or how little we have that defines whether or not our lives are ordinary, but to what degree we are free to say yes to what God is inviting us into.

For me, I had all of the things people associated with the American Dream: a wife, two kids, a million-dollar home, and all the perks that went along with being a self-made man. But I was also stuck, a bond servant to the world I had made. This is not to say the people in my life made me stuck. That is untrue. But the ideas, patterns, and systems that I created became enemies of saying yes. And when it all came crashing down, I was left feeling empty inside. My common life was all about me. What James could do for himself was the hallmark of my life's first act. But as everything began to crack under the strain of my ego, something new was forming in my heart—something that would lead me back to church, back to God, and ultimately into a lifestyle that I had never known before.

Where I thought my life had been about saying yes, I was about to learn that I had been saying no all along. In all my "yeses" to business opportunities that fed my inner desires for wealth and success, I'd left no room for God and the opportunities that he would bring. We call these God-invitations authentic yeses. These are invitations to ideas, behaviors, and opportunities that are in line with God's natural design for our lives. They are authentic because they resonate with our natural giftedness—those talents and abilities that seem to follow us from birth.

When we say yes to anything outside of those things that God has invited us into, we are saying no to his plans and purposes. Such false yeses can feel empowering and exciting at the time but inevitably lead us to feel stuck. Misery is not merely sadness; it is the revelation that we have been going the wrong direction for so long that we don't know how to find our way back. The good news, however, is that we don't need to remain stuck. Learning to identify authentic yes invitations takes hard work, persistence, and humility. But it's possible. And, more than that, it's the only way to truly live the "abundant life" that Jesus came to give us.

Plenty of people live successful lives in the eyes of the world. We are not here to belittle them or naysay their achievements and contributions. Pay honor where it is due. But we are here to say that there is more to living life than just saying yes to yourself. In fact, once you learn to identify and grab ahold of God's yes invitations, no other offers will ever satisfy.

TWO

The Crucible

WHERE YESES ARE BORN

FAR TOO OFTEN, we analyze people who are leading lives of significance and conclude that it's because they were given something at birth that we weren't. Maybe it's physical athleticism that makes them appear superhuman, a trust fund that bankrolls their bigger-than-life endeavor, or a last name that forges a path in arenas that our family name simply won't provide. Some people have that larger-than-life personality we wish we had, or that great body we would die for. Still others, it seems, are always in the right place at the right time. Whatever it is, they got it, and we didn't.

But a quick comparison of the inner worlds of people who are leading lives of significance and those who aren't reveals something much different—that it isn't all about talents, abilities, and connections. Nor is it about good intentions, natural beauty, passionate dreams, or even giftedness. Living an authentic life of significance isn't based on the place you were born, the connections your parents had, or the school you went to.

Instead, the single most important factor in determining our belonging, our usefulness, and our significance is our desire to say yes to God. It's learning to show up to the game ready to play; to embrace the seasons of training as much as the hope of victory against your opponents; and to get involved with plays that move the ball down the field.

Where other people seek to preserve the status quo—no matter what your "normal" looks like to those around—you attempt to do something new, something different. Where other people are intimidated by life's uncertainties, much like Jesus's disciples were scared by the storm that assaulted his fishing craft in Matthew 14, you step out of the boat to answer a divine call like Peter.

Saying yes to new opportunities is not only a skill you can learn but, like all skills, one you can improve over time. At first, it may feel perplexing and downright scary. Venturing into unknown territory is not for the faint of heart. Not everyone in America's first east-coast cities was cut out to be a pioneer. But those who were willing to brave the west-bound journey across endless plains and jagged mountains were rewarded with rare opportunities. They decided to embrace the journey while others remained behind.

Where Do Yeses Come From?

Most of us learn how to say no at an early age. If you have ever parented young children, or even witnessed a toddler at a family member's or friend's house, you know that a child's no-response can create tension-filled and even hostile encounters. From a refusal to eat food to not wanting to come off the playground, parents and children can get into screaming matches over this clash of wills—much to the chagrin of onlookers who have to suffer through the very public and very awkward fallout.

For good parents, however, a child's no-response provides a powerful teaching moment. In it, they can define healthy behaviors that result in life-giving consequences. They can also use the lessons to warn against unhealthy actions that result in damaging effects—both for the child and those the child is in relationship with.

This fundamental teaching, one often lost amidst the shouting matches of exhausted parents and children, is the groundwork we need in our adult lives to identify and say yes to God's greatest invitations for us. Like a good parent who really does know what's best for us, God is uniquely qualified to see every outcome, from beginning to end, and know just how we will fit into that equation.

Likewise, and far more critical than mere situational assessments, God knows us better than we know ourselves. While we can certainly discern our own desires, God knows them far better.

No, this is not the point in the book where we will say something trivial like, "God will change your desires to become his desires." The noble longings of your heart were already placed there by God to begin with, and he likes that. This is not to say he won't refine our wants and purify our character in the process. But it is to say that God isn't in some sort of exchange business where he's trying to take you for all you're worth just to shortchange you with something you hate.

Deep inside you, those things about life that you love—he loves those things too. The adventure, the discovery, the journey, God is all in with you. After all, he's the one who designed you, who knit you together in your mother's womb, and who created you with ambitions.

So what does a yes look like? In short, saying yes is the power to recognize, agree with, and charge into the opportunities that God has uniquely created for you. Some are simple—true "no brainers." Others are more complex and even daunting. But all, from the least to the greatest, are tailor-made by him to lead you forward into the beautiful life he desires you to live.

Let this settle in your heart: the best yes opportunities come from God. As Creator of all things, he's aptly suited to make a path for you that is not only conducive to his plans and purposes but tailor-made to suit your heart. There is no person wiser or more powerful than him, which means there is no path more perfect for you than his. We can rightly conclude, then, that every opportunity God brings you is the best opportunity. Every person he wants you to meet, every step he asks you to take in faith, and every idea he invites you to steward all fall under the same category: *the best.*

Before you start asking, "Yes, but how do I know which opportunities are from him and which aren't?" we cannot emphasize enough the need to recognize his superiority in penning your ultimate destiny. This is not merely an exercise in trying to reinforce your trust in him—which is undoubtedly part of our agenda. Believing that God has your best interests in mind can often be a years-long conversion of the heart. Instead, we want it to sink in deep that all of God's ideas for you, from the least to the greatest, are the best at their proper time, and every alternative is just a no disguised as a yes. You can choose those cleverly disguised noes in yes clothing, but they will never satisfy the way divine yeses can.

From the Ashes

Learning to recognize God's invitations into a life of yes and spot counterfeit opportunities is a valuable skill. It is worth noting that the more often (and the more quickly) we learn to say yes to God moments, the more heaven brings additional opportunities for us. One yes is permission for the next yes. But this is not the best place to start looking for yes moments. The epicenter for the most meaningful yeses of our lives usually comes from the place we are least looking for them.

From our pain.

For me, Sarah, my pain was knowing that I was meant for more—meant to serve others and not just myself. There was a deep dissatisfaction, a loneliness of soul that could not be cured by working harder or smarter. Something inside me was dying, and I needed a new life. I needed a change.

In our western comfort-driven society, we often bristle at the first signs of pain. We can be so risk-averse that we never step foot into the necessary conflicts that will ultimately shape who the world needs us to become. Instead, we moan and complain, too afraid to engage in the hard work of suffering. But it's precisely this suffering that leads us to something beautiful—to significant yes opportunities from God.

The apostle Paul, the famed leader of the first church, warned us against suffering poorly when he said, "do all things without grumbling" (Philippians 2:14). The implication wasn't whether or not we suffered—suffering was expected—but how we walked through the dark seasons of life.

Likewise, we believe that how we suffer is also just as important as what we suffer through. Plenty of people go through pain. There's probably not a person alive who doesn't know some measure of physical, emotional, or mental anguish. It's part of the human experience. And yet, knowing that, the New Testament writer James still asked the earliest Christians to "consider it pure joy" when they suffered all manner of trials (James 1:2).

And for what? Is such endurance simply so that we might be able to offer the world some toolbox of trivial anecdotes? "Look at me. I went through hardship and managed to keep a smile on my face." Or does it serve a deeper purpose?

James goes on to say that such "joyful suffering" ultimately produces a type of perfection that, when forged from endurance, results in maturity and faith. And it is precisely this kind of fire-forged faith that positions us to encounter some of our most profound yes opportunities.

FOR ME, James, my greatest pain stemmed from the financial and relational hits that set me back in 2007. I was forced to sell off all my full-service restaurants to pay the mounting debts I had incurred. Despite all my hard work and ingenuity, I not only saw how far young James could take himself when pursuing his own interests, but I also came face to face with young James's limitations—and he hit those limits, hard. As my first marriage fell apart and I tried sorting through the ashes of those failed businesses, I realized that this was not the life I wanted to live. Like Sarah, I was meant for more.

While I climbed free of my debts, I made a living by hanging on to my Burger King restaurants. Likewise, I filed for divorce and worked like crazy to support my two children. It was during this tumultuous season that several things happened, the first of which was meeting Sarah.

Sarah had become a manager at one of my Burger King stores. She'd been assigned to help me by her brother, Steve, who was a general manager. The connection couldn't have come at a better time for me as not only did I need assistance from influential people around me (a point we'll discuss later), but I needed God back in my life. Sarah, like me, was brought up in the church, and, like me, she had taken a hiatus from her spiritual walk—but never her awareness of God's presence.

While we wouldn't be married for several years, the time together helped redirect my priorities; namely, that I needed to put Jesus first. The Burger Kings flourished under Sarah's and my partnership, and I was able to get clear of financial burdens and faithfully take care of my kids. And when Sarah and I decided to get married in June of 2013, we knew the blessings that were coming our way weren't accidental, nor were they merely because of our ingenuity or hard work—I'd already learned that lesson the hard way. The blessings we were experiencing were coming from God.

Hidden in the tragedy of my divorce and failed restaurants was the most important key to discovering what it meant for me, James, to live a life of saying yes. I needed to learn how to wait on God.

Whereas before, young James was all about ego, speed, high-octane efficiency, and what *he* could do, the new James emerging from the ashes of defeat was discovering what *God* could do. He was learning to slow down and think—not about what plans James could come up with, but what plans God already had in mind. This new awareness of his presence, of his strategic focus on life and how it was to be lived, began to possess me. You might say it was a holy preoccupation. I had seen the power of what I could accomplish, and it had ended poorly. Now it was time to see what God could accomplish.

It was in this season of rebuilding that both of us learned

about the power of failure, pain, and loneliness. There is something beautiful about coming to the end of yourself, of experiencing significant loss, of enduring deep brokenness. God seems to love to use those temporary weaknesses as opportunities to allow his glory to shine through. It was in these dark moments that we learned a valuable truth: your next yes is most likely hunting you down in the wreckage of your past mistakes.

If things seem like they're burning down around you, be encouraged. The most fertile soil comes from fire. There's a reason such lush vegetation grows out of ancient lava beds. So if you're interested in maturing in your relationship to God or being used in significant ways, be prepared to watch some things burn. No, we don't mean for you to become sadists. But we do want to encourage you that any suffering you're currently facing is most likely your permission to enter into seeing new yes opportunities for the first time. Pain is not the end. Instead, suffering means there's a significant purpose for your future. Hardship happens whether or not we want it, but personal transformation comes when we invite it.

THREE

Leaning Toward God

ONE OF THE big mistakes people often make during dark seasons of the soul is that of blaming God for the situations they have gone through or the pain they are experiencing. It is easy to understand why. The very idea of God, whether you are a Christian or not, is that he is in control of everything. God has it all in the "palm of his hand." Consequently, this means that when everything goes south, God is the easiest one to blame.

The problem with this position, of course, is that it eliminates humanity from the equation. Chiefly, if God is responsible for everything, then it doesn't matter what we do, because he's always more powerful than we are.

Worse still is that we can't find this view in Scripture, nor do we find it in nature. What we see instead is the idea that God has made the whole world for us, his prized creations, and given us agency in the world to do with it as we please. This dates back to the beginning of the Bible, where God made humanity, declared us good, and then gave us stewardship of the earth and all that happens in it (see Genesis 1–3). In other words, by God's design, life and its consequences are in our hands as faithful stewards.

But rather than remove himself entirely from his relationship with humanity, God sets himself up as counsel for us, someone we can turn to. Like the psalmist, we can choose to say, "I call on you, my God, for you will answer me" (Psalm 17:6).

It is in this divine heaven-to-earth relationship that we find the two key players who drive the direction of our lives. The first is the individual self, complete with desires, a free will, and the ability to make decisions that have consequences. The second is God, who has desires, a free will, and the ability to make decisions that have consequences. Any relationship without two able-bodied independent people working in mutually beneficial ways is not a relationship, but a dysfunctional mess.

A key point to understand here is that God has already taken the initiative to lean toward us. Meaning, the mere fact that he made us, loved us, and gave us agency to determine our futures demonstrates that he is uniquely interested in knowing who we are and what we want. But like any relationship, it can become lopsided if we are not careful. Namely, that only one party seems interested in moving the relationship forward.

Unfortunately, this is often our approach to God. While he is interested in what we want in life, we couldn't care less about what he wants. This attitude sums up who we, James and Sarah, both were before the bottom fell out of our best attempts to control our lives. We hadn't involved God, refusing to invite him into our plans—both out of arrogance and ignorance.

Leaning Like Heaven

As the smoke cleared from our individual failures, there was a new offer on the table, one we hadn't seen before. It was the offer to reciprocate God's leaning in toward us by leaning toward him. Just as we played a critical role in our failures, God wanted and longed for the opportunity to play a crucial role in our successes.

We call this the principle of leaning into God.

Rather than blame him, our job is to recognize him. Whether it's in subtle ways, like attributing seemingly innocuous blessings to his divine genius, or big ways, like demonstratively praying for his active wisdom and guidance in decision-making, we are called to invite God into our plans. We believe that no Christian can afford *not* to invite God into his or her strategy sessions. The psalmist agreed, making a very bold statement: "Ask the Lord to bless your plans, and you will be successful in carrying them out" (Proverbs 16:3 [GNT]). The inverse can rightly be assumed: "Don't ask God to bless your plans, and you won't have the strength to pull any of them off."

After we got married, we started going back to church together. This was our first physical act of leaning back into God. We wanted to be around his people and discover his plans for us, so church just made sense. But rather than attend church with the attitudes we'd had as children—going only because our parents went, because we had to, or because we were going to hell if we didn't—we went with a new purpose in mind. We went to church to lean into God and put what we learned into practice.

For over a decade beforehand, we had gone to church individually and never once moved the needle forward for Jesus. There was nothing in us as people that said, "Now we're really going to do something for Christ and help build his kingdom." Rather, it was a religious act of going through the motions. But this time would be different. This time we went expecting to meet with God, and eager to know what he had in store for us. We didn't want to take up space in the seats. Instead, we wanted to take action and engage with whatever the Holy Spirit told us to do. Our attitude from day one was "Big, bold, blind faith." Little did we know how far that simple mantra would take us.

In years past, many well-meaning people told us that Jesus would "make everything better." While that sounds nice—the epitome of a Christian Hallmark card—it felt far too akin to the earlier assertion we mentioned that removed one person from the relationship. Plus, we didn't see Jesus as our "quick fix" agent. We saw him as God of the heavens and the earth. His job was not to "make everything better" in our lives. Instead, our job was to reciprocate the "leaning in" that we already felt from his side of heaven. Trusting that Jesus will "make everything better" not only provides a false sense of hope, but it leads capable people to believe they don't have a valuable part to play in moving forward in life. Rather, we are commissioned to answer God's call on our lives with as much energy and passion as we can muster.

This is the heartbeat behind living a life of yes.

At the core, a yes-life recognizes God's incredible gift of life and responds with an emphatic proclamation of, "Whatever you want to do, I'm in." It is as if God has handed you a white sheet of paper with a signature line at the bottom. Then he asks you to sign your name, leaving him to fill in the blank space. It takes nerves of steel—until we realize this is precisely what the life of faith looks like. And seeing it is made even easier when we remember that God only has our absolute best in mind. Further still, he only wants to bring about the desires of our hearts, not crush them. It's as if that blank sheet of paper has something written in bold print on the backside: Special Projects: The Desires of the Heart.

Getting the Heart Right

I, James, remember growing up and singing songs in the church as a kid. Both Sarah and I were raised in legalistic churches, ones that seemed to prize morality as a Gospel unto itself, not the good news of God's love for humanity. Somewhere along the line, this message of love was hijacked by rules and regulations. So the songs were empty for me.

When we finally decided to get back to church, I found myself mouthing the words to the songs, not singing them. I had too many bad memories from my past that prevented me from connecting these worship songs to the God I thought I knew.

But something was happening in my heart. God was happening.

This practice of mouthing the words during Sunday services went on for a while until one day, my heart began to open toward Jesus. Suddenly, the words started to make sense, and I wasn't comparing God to the religion of my youth, I was connecting him to the salvation of my present. And I wept. I finally understood Christ's unconditional love for me, that no matter what had happened in my past, he loved me as I was and would take me as I was. This was not the legalistic church of my youth, where I had to get everything right so that God would love me. God loved me, and I would be empowered to make things right.

Several vital decisions came from this new season of leaning into God. The first was that neither of us would ever make a business decision again without inviting God into the process and listening for his voice to speak and give direction. We didn't see this as a magic cure-all, just as we didn't believe he would do all the hard work for us. Alternatively, we acknowledged that the Holy Spirit had a rightful place at the table in the relationship we were forming together. We agreed with King Solomon of Israel when he quilled the famous line, "A cord of three strands is not quickly broken" (Ecclesiastes 4:12).

Another critical choice was that we would never again make decisions—personal or business—out of greed or egotism. We had seen the destruction that such pursuits brought, and we never wanted to go back. Instead, we asked that whatever we were given stewardship of, he would show us ways to utilize those things, whether restaurants or riches, to bring him glory.

But perhaps the most valuable and enduring decision we made was that we would be a worshipping family. To truly worship God, there must be a constant element of surrender. This is not some strange exercise in which God somehow needs praise to feel good about himself. Instead, it is the simple acknowledgement that he is God, and we need his presence if we are to live life God's way. Perhaps even more than that, it is an act of submitting to his heart as he has miraculously entrusted his heart to us.

Moving Forward in Worship

If yes opportunities are birthed from ashes, worship is the fuel that keeps the fires burning. And, no, not the fires of destruction. Instead, these are the fires of passion that burn in the hearts of Christians who engage in the activities that delight

God's heart. And if anything delights his heart, trust us: it will most certainly delight our hearts too.

As we chose to worship God and redirect all our efforts toward saying yes to whatever he wanted to come out way, the most remarkable things began to happen. Unexpected things. Heavenly things.

The first was the feeling of pure contentment in our marriage and our home. Where previous relationships were marked with strife, bickering, and restlessness, our focus on putting Jesus first precipitated the kind of fruit mentioned in Galatians (5:22-23). The practice of worshipping God—whether through singing songs in church and around our house, or by the worshipful acts of obedience that accompany Christians endeavoring to lead Godly lives—our hearts began to open up to his heart.

This happens much the same way an old analog antenna picks up radio waves. The first radios had big dials that allowed an operator to sweep through a range of frequencies to find the desired broadcast frequency. But more often than not, most of the searching was spent sweeping through static. This was very much what it was like during the years of our common lives. We spent a lot of time in the static.

But in the age of digital music, there's no more static. Everything is preset and ready to go. All a user needs to do is open the app or fire up the in-vehicle subscription service, and —voila—there's audio content right at our fingertips. This is what a worshipping attitude did for us. It transformed us from individuals who were moving about aimlessly under our own power to a super-charged couple who had unlimited access to God's heart—all we needed to do was ask.

If you're in a place where life seems foggy and you're unsure what's God and what's not, we want to encourage you to take on the posture and practice of a worshipping Christian. This means thanking him for everything in your life, from little to big. This also means learning to submit your heart to him in prayer and singing. No, your prayer life won't look like everyone else's, but you must communicate with him. And, nope, you don't have to be the greatest singer to engage in a musical worship service, but you must be pressing in with your passion. Nothing clarifies the heart of a person like worshiping God. Try it and see for yourself.

The second thing that happened was that favor started following us. Many people would call this good luck, but luck can't be this intentional or thoughtful. No, such fortuitous happenings could only come from a person—namely, the Holy Spirit.

This favor took the form of new restaurants that God, seemingly, wanted us to steward. The opportunities were often quite unexplainable, as in, we hadn't done anything special to deserve them. We simply tried to be faithful to what God had already given us and worshipped him through the process.

Burger King Corporation, for example, called us with invitations to acquire several new stores. One restaurant was in a mall with high volume foot traffic. We couldn't have asked for a better location. Even stores that, on initial examination, were performing very poorly in seemingly bad locations turned out to be stores that we knew how to turn around. One Burger King, in particular, turned out to be smack-dab in the middle of 18,000 homes within a one-mile radius, but no one under the previous management knew how to reach those homes. We did and completely turned the restaurant around.

This season of favor taught us another principle: that God will never give you the next thing until you demonstrate proficiency with the present thing. So often Christians want a promotion from God—a spouse, a raise, a move. There's nothing inherently wrong with any of those things, and it's easy to believe that a good God would love any of his children to have such virtuous things. However, because he is a God of order (1 Corinthians 14:33), he tends not to give us the next job until we show we can steward the present one. One of the ways we learn to identify yes opportunities is by being faithful to the last opportunity God gave us, and worship him because of it and through it.

This is also good parenting. No mom or dad asks their daughter or son to finish basic math and then jump straight into quantum physics. We learn and grow progressively because that's how God designed us to learn and grow. So why would he ever break that foundational aspect of our development simply to answer some crazy prayer that would only serve to damage us? The answer is, he won't. Sometimes, the prayers we're praying are the prayers he's not going to answer.

If you feel stuck, try going to God in prayer and spending

some time in quiet self-examination. Consider when you started feeling stuck, and then look back to see if you can spot the last set of marching orders God gave you. More than likely, it's those very same orders that he's looking for you to be faithful with before your next promotion. Contrary to what our hearts may scream out for, this is not God holding us back because he doesn't want us to succeed, but this is God holding us back to keep us from failing in unrecoverable ways. Sometimes, a lack of advancement is mercy in disguise.

Another thing we noticed amid our new worship-oriented lifestyle was that we were pushing a lot less. One of the things we did in our younger years was strive for success. This is not to be confused with hard work or perseverance. Instead, striving is exerting emotional energy in areas that you have no natural grace or gifting in. It's the overcommitment that feeds the ego rather than an honest response that humbly recognizes limitations and honors legitimate expectations.

As we were offered more opportunities, we decided not to push any doors open or insist that anything happen. We took a relaxed posture, one that said, "God, if you want this to happen, we're ready to work and apply ourselves, but only if you bring it about." Notice that our "relaxed posture" did not exclude hard work. Many people get this wrong, thinking that waiting on God means you can freeload your way through life. That's bogus. Instead, we reaffirmed our desire to God that we would work just as diligently with new opportunities as we would with previous prospects, but it was he who had to be the one to create those "ways in the wilderness" (Isaiah 43:19).

So often, we Christians can get in our own way. We muddy the waters by running after things that God never invited us to pursue. Note, again, that the primary way we recognize what is him and what is not has everything to do with learning to worship him. If Jesus said that his "sheep hear his voice," then the primary way we learn to hear his voice is not busying ourselves with constant activity—no matter how spiritual it may appear—but by learning to rest, wait on, and worship him.

Unless we *know*, unless we see God's hand pushing a door open and hear his voice saying, "This is the way," we're staying put. We refuse to chop the door down with an ax—it has to be open on its own.

Many people get in trouble here. They misappropriate the presence of a door for the invitation to walk through that door. In reality, there are doors of opportunity around us all the time, every day. If we were called to walk through every door we encountered, we'd be basket cases! That's no way to live life.

If you feel exhausted at the moment, try to assess how many doors you've walked through in the past few weeks, months, and years. And then, with the Holy Spirit's help, ask how many of those were his leading and how many were you taking a battle ax to the opportunity. The fact is, you don't need all the headaches that come with doors you were never meant to walk through. No one does. Life can be tough enough as it is—leave those headaches for someone else.

One of two fascinating aspects of walking through doors

that you alone are called to is that you will be uniquely equipped to handle what God brings to you. If you've been around church life much, you may have heard the phrase, "God doesn't call the equipped, he equips the called." While the theological nuances of such a statement can be argued over, the sentiment that the Holy Spirit will enable you to walk into the opportunities he's formed for you is genuine.

The second beautiful aspect of walking through doors that you alone are called to is that God "rewards those who diligently seek him" (Hebrews 11:16). This means that in heaven's economy, rewards arrive in conjunction with our diligent pursuit of God's heart. Again, we didn't know it at the time, but as we pressed into God through worship, we were actually setting ourselves up for rewards. This simple biblical precedent transcends language, culture, and economy. It will preach in every country on the planet. It's a universal divine truth that you can bank on. Wherever there is worship, there is always opportunity and reward.

FOUR

Buckle Up

I'VE ALWAYS HAD a thing for cars. Yeah, me—James. In my younger years, they suited the bigger-than-life persona I was building for myself. But just as Sarah and I were moving into a season of immense transformation with God, I recognized that, like fast cars, with great power comes great responsibility.

My passion for supercars led me to take professional driving lessons. Video games make novices think they know what it's like to sit behind the wheel of a 480-horse-power beast of a car in real life, but they don't. Learning to drive a high-end vehicle on a closed course takes time, dedication, and talent. Without those qualities, as well as attentive coaching, someone can quickly turn a supercar into a super wreck in the blink of an eye *and* put their life in great peril in the process.

As we discussed in the previous chapter, God is progressional in how he builds us. Once he finds that we are leaning into him, he takes his time with entrusting us with greater and greater responsibilities that impact more and more people. As with the progression of going from scooter to bicycle, go-kart to first car, and fast car to a supercar, God is methodical in how he prepares us for "greater works" (John 14:12).

So what is the secret sauce for learning how to go faster?—because we all want to go faster, right? What is the thing that qualifies us for moving to the next stage?

Yes, as previously discussed, faithfulness and competency have a great deal to do with showing God and others what they can expect from us. But just as there is a heartbeat behind every act of worship, there is also a heartbeat behind leveling up.

This Car Has More Than One Gear

Cars have gears for a reason. While that may seem obvious to everyone who's ever driven one, the mechanics behind it are essential to making an engine work for you (and not against you).

Without gears, everyone would be traveling the same speed all the time on every road in every condition. Not only would that be extremely frustrating, but it would also be downright dangerous. Instead, long ago, engineers developed ways to accommodate for variations in speed while still asking the engine to do the same amount of work. The result is something we take for granted every day.

Learning to say yes is a lot like learning to use the different gears of a car. And the more adept we become at knowing how each one works and how to apply them, the more efficiently we can drive and get to where we need to go.

As previously discussed, the need to recognize God as the source of all things and adopt a genuine lifestyle of worship could easily be considered first gear. Without it, we're not going anywhere. But coming in at number two is the gear of gratitude.

Gratitude isn't just about saying thanks to people who give you stuff. Instead, it is a profound sense of appreciation for even the most mundane aspects of our lives. At its core, it's the pure thankfulness we find in being alive. And you probably know a few people like this. Sometimes, they can seem annoying or even fake. It's almost as if they're always high on life, looking at the world with childlike wonder-filled eyes. But the more you spend time around genuinely grateful people, the more you realize they're not disingenuous—they're tapping into a way of living that makes you jealous.

Grateful people seem to appreciate things everyone else takes for granted, and they inspire others to be more attentive to the little things in life. Grateful people exude a near-constant aura of immense appreciation to the point that it almost seems ridiculous. But in their ridiculousness, they've discovered two of heaven's best kept secrets.

The first is that gratitude makes us strong.

A beautiful Old Testament scripture says that God's eyes "range throughout the earth to strengthen those whose hearts are fully committed to him" (2 Chronicles 16:9). Then Paul writes to the New Testament church, challenging them to "give thanks in all circumstances; for this is God's will for you in Christ Jesus" (1 Thessalonians 5:18). The connection point between the passages comes when we recognize that when we're behaving gratefully—because it's what Jesus desires for us—we end up finding supernatural strength for everything else we face.

We demonstrate commitment to God by thanking him all the many blessings around us, great and small. It means we look at lightbulbs in our bathroom and thank him. We thank him for running water that we can drink without fear of becoming sick—most of our toilet water is cleaner than the rest of the world's drinking water! When we see the tires on our car, we thank him. When we see a postage stamp, we thank him.

Yes, it seems tiring, over the top, and maybe even a bit psychotic—until we realize we have far more to be grateful for than to complain about. The most influential people we have ever known are the most grateful; conversely, the weakest people we've ever met are spoiled, entitled, unappreciative, and reckless.

The second secret is that gratitude is the gatekeeper of provision.

All three tellings of the parable of the faithful servant (Matthew 24:42-51, Mark 13:34-37, and Luke 12:35-48) share a similar theme about the person who takes care of the master's property well: they obtain more material resources for which to be responsible. And while someone may argue that faithfulness is the gatekeeper of provision—which it certainly is—gratitude is the heart behind it. Gratitude says, "Master, I am humbled that you would even entrust something of yours to me in the first place, and I pray that I am worthy of the blessing." Gratitude is the thing that motivates us to be faithful to God because we can't even believe he saw fit to choose us in the first place.

And it is precisely this kind of person who the Holy Spirit loves to draw near to and strengthen. It's this person who is touching the heart of heaven and can be trusted with its riches—not because they are the smartest or brightest or best looking, but because they are inviting the character of God to reform their worldview. "This one, right here," God says. "This one, we can trust."

Remember, gratitude is sacred. It originates from heaven itself, and when we start operating with an attitude of gratitude, we are inviting heaven's atmosphere to draw near to us.

We invite you to try gratitude out. And not just on the good days when everything is going well, but especially on the hard days when it isn't. If the radiator breaks, make sure to take a second and thank the Holy Spirit for the tires. If the washing machine quits, thank God that the dryer is still going. We are convinced that if you begin thanking God for what's working, he'll attend to what is not.

Now What, God?

As God began blessing us with new stores to steward, we started seeing incredible returns on our investments. We're talking returns that quite literally left us speechless because the profitability of our work was staggering. For every $100,000 we made, we were putting $20,000 of that in the bank. You don't have to be a brainiac at math to know those are some great looking numbers.

But rather than bask in the glory of those earnings and pat ourselves on the back, we knew a kingdom-minded response was required of us. Put simply, we knew that even with all of our hard work, ingenuity, and experience, this much financial success wasn't because of us—it was because God was breathing on our lives.

Whenever you start to sense God breathing on something in your life, the most significant single act of worship you can offer is to ask the question we asked him when all this was going down: what can we do with all that you've given us to glorify you?

Of course, the infancy of this question is prefaced by an even more innocent request: God, why are you blessing us? But the answer to that one was more simple than we recognized. God's reply to us is the same as it was to Abram: God blesses us so that we might be a blessing to others (see Genesis 12:1–2).

It's no more complicated than that, but no less profound. You are blessed to be a blessing.

Yes, learning to step out in faith and sign your name on that blank sheet of paper can be scary. But once you do and start living a life of yes to God, you position yourself to answer one of the greatest questions of all: now that we're here, what can we do for others?

No matter your vocation, occupation, net worth, or individual capacities, recognizing that you have something to offer those around you is, without a doubt, one of the most rewarding and personally gratifying discoveries you can ever make.

Where life truly began to accelerate for us was at the intersection of asking God what we could do and responding to yes opportunities. These two distinct and very dynamic heavenly virtues were building momentum in our lives, preparing to launch us into places we could never have imagined.

On the heels of asking God, "Now what?" we had a series of opportunities to serve others. Someone in desperate need came to us requesting help with a mortgage. It was a debt we were able to cover, and we knew God had brought the person into our lives "for such a time as this" (Esther 4:14). Another time, a church contacted us, asking for help with purchasing an expensive HVAC unit for their sanctuary. They had been struggling through months of fundraising, and we were able to secure the unit in a single day. Sometimes our desire to bless people bubbled over to the point that we would do crazy and adventurous things. On one occasion, we handed out hundreds of cheeseburgers to hungry people on the streets—some impoverished, others not—all of whom were blessed to get a simple sandwich for free.

The secret we discovered was that the gift-giving and generosity helped keep our perspective on Jesus and off two people who we didn't want to meet again—the old James and Sarah. We refused to get selfish again, to the point that we even had a holy fear of returning to the past. We knew the stench of that lifestyle all too well, and we wanted none of it. Instead, we wanted to embrace every opportunity from God to say yes to serving others.

Perhaps more astounding than anything else, however, was the reality that we kept landing in the middle of God's favor and provision. We'd heard Christian leaders say things like, "You can't out-give God," or, "If you're faithful, you won't be able to stop blessings from following you." For us, those seemed like hocus-pocus fairy words. It was just a bunch of fake people talking big.

Until it happened to us.

We found that as we did our very best to be faithful to every yes invitation we received, more blessings seemed to follow us home like little lost puppies. Before long, we had so many puppies we had to orient our lives around giving them away just to keep from being overrun. And there's a crazy thought—being overrun with blessings! Do your very best not to read "Prosperity Gospel" into that statement. Instead, read, "because that's heaven." As it turns out, heaven really does desire to hunt us down.

What do we mean by this?

Sometimes, you don't even know that you're being blessed when you're acting generously.

One day, we decided to bless four pastors with $2,500 gifts each. Mind you, pastors are some of the hardest-working, most underpaid people on the planet. If you ever have the opportunity to do something special for them, don't think twice—don't even pray about it—just do it.

The day after we gave the anonymous gifts, we got word that through a series of miraculous circumstances that we would be able to save $100,000 on a major business deal. The timing between blessing those pastors and receiving the savings was too uncanny to deny. But rather than pocket the money, we decided to do something really crazy—we gave the $100,000 away.

We don't care who you are—giving $100,000 away is a big deal, no matter your annual revenue or net worth. But we both realized that the same principles that applied to us before applied to us now, and they were embodied in that prayer: "God, what can we do with all that you've given us to glorify you?"

So, over the next three months, we gave away $100,000, sowing it into a Christian ministry that we sensed we were supposed to bless.

And then things got even crazier—so much so that we wouldn't believe unless we'd lived it. The very next day, we received the opportunity to make an offer on a forty-seven-store deal. That is, to purchase forty-seven restaurants in a single agreement.

Today, we laugh, thinking about how astonished we were when presented that news. But, at the same time, we smile, knowing that God was in the middle of showing off and proving that the ways of his kingdom are not our ways. The world's model says, "Horde it all. Keep it. Sit on it. And shoot anyone who tries to take it." But God's kingdom-model says, "God has entrusted this to you for a purpose, and he has a whole world in need of your care. So, if you'll be faithful, if you'll learn to say yes and resist the temptation of living the common life, God wants to use you to do some pretty off the hook stuff. Are you ready? Because it's time to buckle up."

Learn to handle small yeses well—they are the gatekeepers to bigger ones.

Perhaps you are wondering where all the "significant opportunities" are in your life? They might be lurking in the shadows of the invitations to obedience that you overlooked.

We want to challenge you not to miss the chance to say yes. Divine yes opportunities are all around you. They are everywhere, every day—some so small you might miss them if you blink, and others so big you'll need a hit of oxygen before you attempt summiting the mountain. Learning to worship Jesus daily, combined with a deep desire to bless others out of your overflow, will position you to say yes and keep on saying yes in incredible ways.

FIVE

Is This Happening?

"THERE'S GOT to be something more than this."

Have you ever had that thought run through your head? Have you ever thought there must be something more significant to life than your present experience? It's like you wake up one day, look into the same mug of coffee, look out the same kitchen window, and think, "Is this it?" That's not to say there is anything wrong with consistency or predictability; faithfulness and perseverance are kingdom attributes.

What we are talking about is a restlessness of soul that makes you uneasy when faced with the prospect of hitting the proverbial glass ceiling. You have reached as high as you will ever go; there is nothing further. It's the end of the line. Thanks for playing.

Despite all our external wealth and success, by May of 2015, we prayed the very disruptive prayer that we mentioned in the last chapter—"You've blessed us. So now what?" But it was more than just what to do with all the blessings we'd received. It was about finding a deeper purpose in those blessings. And that purpose had everything to do with how we wanted to spend our time.

Believe it or not, the most impressive thing to people of wealth and power is not how much money someone has. It's how they spend their time. Money can be made and lost in seconds, but time is the only commodity that genuinely matters. We cannot make more of it, and we cannot get back that which has already been spent.

We realized that the restlessness of our hearts was not merely how to give away the material blessings God had given us but how to spend our time. What was more, we didn't have any clue what it was going to be. And that thought is more unsettling than anyone can know until you're looking at the blank sheet of paper for yourself. "What is God going to write across it?" you ask yourself, nervously fretting about the future content. "What will he ask of me?"

As hours turn into days, and days into weeks, the anxiety of anticipation builds until you reach a new set of questions, ones that are, perhaps, even more terrifying than the first: "What if God doesn't write anything on the paper? Or what if I can't read it or hear his voice? Or what if it's too hard?"

Then, when you least expect it, the phone rings.

When God calls

For us, God answered our prayer in an unlikely way—though, that seems to be his modus operandi much of the time. He's not called Jehovah Sneaky by accident. (No, don't try looking that up in your Hebrew study guide).

Thirty days after we began praying the "Now what?" prayer, I, James, received a phone call that would change my life. I had just finished a round of golf at a beautiful resort when my cell phone rang at our dinner table.

"Hello?" I said.

"Jamie?"

"Yeah?" I looked at Sarah.

"Who is it?" she asked.

"It's an old friend," I said. "From high school."

"High school?"

Sure enough, this particular classmate, who I'll call Jeff, and I had not spoken with one another in thirty-some years. So to get a call from him now was indeed an "out of the blue" happening.

He and I didn't chitchat for long. In fact, my old classmate pretty much led with the very last question I ever would have seen coming. "Would you like to go to Haiti?"

At that moment, something strange happened. My usual analytical self, the one that built restaurants, managed hundreds of employees, reviewed contracts, and went toe to toe with attorneys, responded without even thinking.

I repeated the question to Sarah, and then we both said, "Yes."

The very next thought that went through both of our heads was, "Oh, crap."

What had we just said yes to?

We hadn't the faintest clue!

We knew nothing about what my old classmate did or what we'd just signed up for. But on the heels of the dangerous prayers that we'd been praying, something about this phone call didn't sound like a man inviting us to Haiti. It felt like God.

Prayer, it's often said, doesn't move God. It moves us. Furthermore, we have found that being able to say yes to God, and discerning what invitations are from him and what aren't, has to do with the posture of our hearts in prayer. Dangerous prayers have a way of moving us so close the Father's heart that we can't help but hear him when he speaks. When you're that close to Jesus's bosom, resting your head on him as John did in John 13:23, you're going to hear his heartbeat. And even if you're deaf, you'll feel it. God always makes sure his children hear his voice if they are, indeed, longing to encounter him (John 10:27). And we were.

―――

OVER THE COMING WEEKS, as we learned about Jeff's missions work in Haiti, we started to educate ourselves. For me, Sarah, I knew that I didn't want us going into a trip blind. I wanted to make sure we were aware of the culture, the political climate, and the needs of the people. So we read everything we could about Haiti. We watched videos, made phone calls, and kept notes.

By the time our trip rolled around, we knew we were going to a very needy nation, one racked by political unrest, natural disasters, endless violence, and economic chaos. We also knew we were walking into tremendous spiritual depravity. As famed photographer Lynne Warberg once said, "Haitians are 70 percent Catholic, 30 percent Protestant, and 100 percent voodoo."[1]

Perhaps had we known about all this in advance, we wouldn't have said yes to Jeff so readily. Maybe we would have allowed our apprehensions about visiting the most impoverished nation in the western hemisphere to jade our response to Jeff.[2] Who knows. And it's because of these suppositions that we believe God often hides our future for us, not from us. Were we to see the story in advance, there's a high likelihood we would not have taken the path. The risks seemed too dangerous, the costs, too high.

If you're in a season of wondering why God is not responding to your prayers with details about what's to come, might we suggest that he could be saving the information for a better day? Remember, he knows us far better than we could ever know ourselves. This means he also knows the best time to clue us in on what he's doing. The key to moving through these "uninformed times" is not to suspect God of malevolent behavior but, instead, to praise him for his mercy. Had we said no to Jeff because of our preconceived ideas about Haiti, we would have missed out on the biggest adventure yet.

Another reason God often appears to delay answering prayer is on account of our impatience. We can be so focused on rushing ahead that we leave everything and everyone else in the dust, including the Holy Spirit. When we feel stuck and are left wondering what to do, we have a tendency to try and push things forward ourselves. Our impatience turns into frustration, which then leads to bad decisions, and then we end up blaming God for the consequences. If you're anything like us, this can be disastrous, hurting you and others you love. Worse still, however, is the fact that we can delay God's answers for our lives.

Getting back on track means slowing down, resisting impatience, and turning our attitude to one of gratitude. It's in a posture of humility that we invite the Holy Spirit to speak to us without any agenda. And if he decides to be silent, that must be okay with us. Remember, when things aren't going your way, there is most likely a very good reason that God has you going through that stage in life. Resist the tendency to rush ahead of God and make a way where he hasn't gone ahead of your first.

One other key for slowing down is pausing to enjoy life's journey. Learning to appreciate where we are in life versus where we wish we were has the amazing side effect of creative gratitude even for the things that don't make sense. Instead of constantly looking at how things "ought" to be, recognize the beauty of the present. This kind of willful appreciation honors the work that God is doing in our lives right now instead of attempting to force him into acting on the new plans that we think he should spend his time on. Not only is the Holy Spirit not moved by such an approach, but it makes us miserable in the process.

Building a Ministry of Yeses

Wisdom to say yes comes progressively, purchased through the habit of being obedient. In the same way that God does not give our next yes opportunity until we've walked through our last one, we must recognize that ministry evolves in much the same way.

By ministry, we mean the formalized system of meeting the spiritual and physical needs of a particular group of people. While some might wince at the use of the word "formal," feeling that it's too limiting or somehow less spiritual, we would point out that without "form" and "formation," we would not have creation, the cross, the resurrection, or the body of Christ—that is, the church. Being formal about something doesn't mean we have to be stodgy and outdated. If anything, it means we can carry more and do more because we took the time to form something of integrity.

Long before we started investing ourselves in ministry in Haiti, we were investing ourselves in other ministry activities. In the last chapter, we described a few instances of how we gave to both individual and group ministry needs. Before we formed a non-profit organization, we were investing in others.

This is an integral part of our journey and, we believe, yours. God was examining how we handled small yes opportunities to see if we could be trusted with larger ones.

Ministry, like life, is evolutionary. It develops over time, maturing with each new lesson learned, each new problem overcome. No ministry that lasts ever begins in the same form that it ends in. Even Jesus's earthly ministry, which started with turning water into wine (John 2:1–11), ended very differently than when it began, with his commissioning of the church (Mark 16:15). But without the wine at the wedding feast, there wouldn't have been resurrection at Calvary. They were a part of the same ministry plan.

Like Jesus's, your ministry today will not look like your ministry tomorrow. And that's good. Development is a sign of health. Being able to see and track growth in your own life is imperative. Likewise, steps of maturity are indicators that you are being faithful with each yes opportunity the Holy Spirit brings to you. Say yes to enough of them, and they have a way of creating their own momentum until you are caring for one after another in quick succession.

You Want Us to Build a What?

The first time we went to Haiti, we were caught entirely off guard. All the research, pictures, stats, and maps cannot prepare anyone for the shock that is Haiti. It's hot, boisterous, and unruly. And yet it's also beautiful and full of wonder. But unless you grew up in a third-world county, and especially if you grew up in middle-class US neighborhoods as we did, Haiti is a total mind-job.

The police are corrupt, the politicians are unscrupulous, the economy is in shambles, and the sense of dysfunction is overwhelming. But more than anything, you are always surrounded by people in need. Never in our lives had we been so close to desperation. We stood elbow to elbow, every hour of the day, with people who had little to nothing in the way of food, clothing, or shelter. And money? It was almost nowhere to be seen.

On that trip, we were asked to a build a school for 125 children in a small community. We had the money to do it. But what we didn't have was the understanding of how such a thing was a "good idea." For me, James, none of what was discussed fit into my brain. It was, to be both proverbial and literal, a hot mess. There was no proposed location for the school, no price for the building, no business model, no materials list—nothing. It went against everything in my head.

Right then, I knew I was coming face to face with another invitation to grow in faith, and another chance to "kill my flesh" in order to see what God might do. I learned that for James to say yes without information requires a real act of God. I like to be in control. I want to see what's going on, then assess it, quantify it, analyze it, and make it more efficient. But this? Building a school without any plan whatsoever? *This is asinine*, I thought to myself. And yet God was there, using his index finger to draw me forward. But for that, I would need help. And I knew just where to turn.

JAMES AND SARAH CAMMILLERI

The Gift of Partnership

One of the first things that I, James, noticed about Sarah when we started working together in business was how much she cared for our employees. And I say that as someone who'd I thought cared about my employees already. But when compared to her? No way. Her sincere acts of kindness overshadowed mine like a blimp blotting out the sun at the Super Bowl.

Where I would send Christmas bonuses to my store managers, thinking I was a good boss, Sarah took it to the next level. She made time to get to know each manager and then, with this knowledge, created hand-made gifts for each of them, which happened to include their bonus check. It was like saying, "Here's how much we appreciate and value you. And, oh yeah, here's a check too." That first year, no one was talking about the extra money they got—they were talking about the gifts Sarah made for them.

SARAH HERE. What James just outlined is all true. However, from my perspective, this felt very natural for me to do. I knew the importance of adding value to people's lives and that it was the only way our company was going to grow. In other words, the power of being a great team doesn't come because everyone has it figured out on their own. If anything, good teams are made up of people who have one part of the puzzle figured out but need others to step in and complete the picture. My normal of making handmade gifts was not normal for James. Likewise, his ability to vision cast was not in my toolbox. But, together, we made a great team.

If you're bumping into particular walls, hitting your head in the same place over and over again, it may be because you can't get past that obstacle with the tools you currently have. Many challenges can be overcome alone, but the most significant ones require help.

WHEN WE WERE ASKED to build that first school, we decided to make use of the partnership we'd already learned to employ in business.

For me, James, I recognized that one of the biggest mistakes I'd made in my previous marriage was not involving my wife in critical decisions. That is a past I can never get back. However, I can allow it to inform my present, and that is the real gift of hindsight. Today, bringing Sarah into all my decision-making is a joy, especially considering how God gave me such a competent and intelligent life partner. I'd be stupid not to invite her into the process! So I decided she would be involved in every decision I made.

Instead of trying to figure this school venture on my own, I turned to Sarah and asked her what she thought. Together, we sought God's direction, and we worked through the details.

Then we went back to the organizers and said, "Yes. Let's do it."

Building that school defied all norms for us. It broke with tradition, laughing in the face of what we knew and how we would have typically gone about doing things. That's when we realized that saying yes to God opportunities tends to draw us out of our comfort zones. By this, we don't mean for you to become reckless or careless in your decision-making—far from it! Instead, it is to say that God knows what he's doing, and sees in advance how he's going to use your obedience to both expand his kingdom and mature you as a person.

In situations like this one about the school, human instinct says, "No." There's no plan, there's no infrastructure, and this country is falling apart at the seams. Heck, there aren't even seams! But maybe, if we have some semblance of discretion and cultural sensitivity, we might reply with, "You know what? We'll think about it."

In prior years, I would have missed out on yes opportunities like this. All the things I said yes to were self-serving, and the things I said no to were about serving others. As previously discussed, what I didn't know back then was that I was saying no to God and no to things that would have benefitted me as a person. That was no way to live, and now I was face to face with the chance to say yes in an entirely new realm—one way outside my comfort zone.

Tests and Their Outcomes

And it doesn't always have to be big yeses that propel us forward. As James and I look back over our business and ministry success, we can see how God used lots of small yeses to build upon one another. Those little acts of obedience led us to start saying yes to even more significant opportunities. Without them, we would never be in the positions we are today. Again, this speaks to God's continuous activity in our hearts and his desire that we grow up in him methodically.

As a result of reflection, we discovered another principle at work in our lives. Before every yes, there's a test.

In the Old Testament book of Judges, there's a story of how God tested Israel to see whether or not they would follow him when the pressure was on (2:21-22). Throughout scripture, we see God doing this sort of thing—not because he's sadistic and or likes to toy with creation; instead, he explained quite clearly what his intent was—"in order to know what was in your heart" (Deuteronomy 8:2). There is something strategic in God's mind about these yes opportunities. They're not *just* about blessing others, but they're about revealing to God what lies on the inside of our hearts. It's as if we are presenting our hearts to him, saying, "Here's what's going on in me. Take a look and see for yourself."

Saying yes to God invitations has a way of not only showing God what's in us but demonstrating to the watching world what a life surrendered to Christ looks like. And it's beautiful.

The reality is that if we can't learn to handle small yes invitations, we will never be entrusted with big ones—no matter how much glory we think God would be getting if they came out that way. The following example may sound trite, but it is no less accurate: If you don't know how to steward $500 wisely, no loving person—let alone God—would ever unnecessarily burden you with the responsibilities that come with stewarding $500,000. We know because we've lived it, seeing both sides of the obedience coin. We cannot receive a more substantial sum without stewarding the smaller. The lesser amount proves to be the more significant one too, at least in terms of determining the initial attitude of our heart, since it is the test before the yes.

Yeses aren't always about finances, either (though discussing money does tend to cut to most people's hearts faster than any other topic). When you think of someone, reach out to them with a call or text. More often than not, it's God trying to get your attention. When you're in the grocery store and sense the Holy Spirit tugging on your heart to speak to a person in the checkout line, give it a shot. The words may not be quite right, but your heart will be. And if you have the chance to do something neighborly, and you sense God breathing on the idea in ways you can't explain, act on it, if for no other reason than to see what happens.

Learning to be sensitive to the Holy Spirit's voice is the prerequisite for receiving God's next yes opportunity for you. We encourage you to practice being open and available to what the Holy Spirit might want to say to you or speak through you. It makes every faith decision easier and attracts the attention of heaven.

Remember, expectation is the incubator of opportunity. When we lean into what we hope to see, noticing strategic opportunities becomes much easier.

SIX

Breaking for Haiti

"I CAN USE SOMEONE ELSE HERE," God said to me. "It doesn't have to be you if you don't want it to be."

Never in my life had I, James, been so startled by words from the Holy Spirit, and I knew right then and there that I never wanted him to have to say those words to me again.

By November of 2015, Sarah and I were back in Haiti, standing in the town of Passerine, just outside of Gonaives. As we contemplated whether or not to build a school, we knew that this was our most significant yes moment yet. We both remember feeling overwhelmed as the harsh realities of Haiti struck us, but we believed God had sent us there for a purpose. After all, that was our prayer, wasn't it? "God, now that you've blessed us, what can we do to glorify you?"

It was as if God was saying, "Well, here it is."

But hearing God say that he could use someone else cut me

to the quick. My heart leaped inside my chest with the only response I could think to say. "God, I don't want you to have to ask someone else. Let your eyes stop on us."

Sarah and I had come to a place where we were desperate for God. There was a passion in our hearts that came from a deep place of wanting to do something meaningful for Jesus, even if it didn't make sense. Ironically—or serendipitously, depending on your point of view—nothing about Haiti made sense to us. But it certainly did to God. We had been through so much—had so many tests, so many failures and restarts—that by the time we got to Passerine, the yes opportunity was an easy one to respond to.

Sometimes, we believe people are not ready to say yes in certain areas. It's not because they're bad people, but because they need to go through more—to be pressed more. They haven't yet passed the first yes tests to be faithful with the next yes tests. They're not willing to do the work. And for as hard as we worked for our restaurants in the US, nothing came close to how we would labor in Haiti.

From the Head to the Heart

Our dear friend and mentor, John Maxwell, often asks, "Are you living underwater for Christ?" As a married couple, we decided that our response to such a statement must be, "Yes!" We want to be fully immersed—emotionally, spiritually, and physically, in the work of building God's kingdom. It's what makes us tick. But it comes with a price.

IF THERE WAS EVER a part in the writing of this book where you would see James break down, this is it.

Haiti is a filthy, disorganized mess. It is the polar opposite of how I like to keep my house, my garage, my cars, and my property. Haiti has less in common with James than an NFL quarterback has with a Tibetan monk. And yet, I knew God had called me to help these people, and I couldn't explain why.

But as I observed their lives, now for the second time, something in me broke. In a moment of intense self-reflection, I remember saying to myself, "Look at everything you have that you take for granted, Jamie." I recounted that I had always had a home to live in. I had never gone without food. There were always at least two cars parked in the driveway, and I had plenty of ways to make money in business. I lacked for nothing materially.

I wept, however, as I saw the desperation of a people who earn between $2 and $4 per day—if they're lucky enough to land a job at all. I wept as I realized that almost sixty percent of people live below the poverty line as compared to the United States' twelve percent.[1] I thought I was doing good things before, but in light of everything we were confronted with in Haiti, I said to myself, "You've done nothing, Jamie."

Every American businessperson I've taken to Haiti wants to fix everything. That's an understandable reaction since much of their success comes from solving big problems. But after five years and hundreds of trips to Haiti, we realized it's not our job to fix everything. Moreover, the only person truly capable of fixing Haiti is God, and the people he wants to use the most are the Haitians themselves. Ours is but one part, like a doctor doing triage on the battlefield—those survivors still need a hospital, rehab, and checkups. Eventually, as enough people find health, a collective of humans working through God will indeed be able to touch the mess and make it whole. At the time, I remember thinking that there was nothing we could do to help Haiti. I felt utterly defeated.

The feeling of helplessness only got worse as I grew frustrated with the missions organization we were attached to. I remember sitting through morning devotionals, thinking, "This la-la fru-fru crap is doing *nothing* for the people of Haiti!" I was livid.

Before anyone runs off and calls me a heretic, let me be clear. I did not say "all devotionals are bad," and that "no Christians should ever do them." What I did do, however, was connect personal spiritual development to a lack of physical activity on behalf of needy people in a dire situation. It would be like owning a helicopter transport company and having FEMA ask us to rescue flood victims, but we reply with, "Hold on, we're in a discussion on the book of James and how it might relate to the way we treat our boss."

Worse than that was the fact that I didn't even like the feel of that trip to Passerine. Something just rubbed me the wrong way about being the white Americans who were there to sweep in and save everything. As we will discuss later, it's this very attitude that has ended up harming Haiti, not helping it.

I found myself surrounded by who I viewed as self-righteous camp counselors trying to make themselves feel good about being in Haiti but doing nothing to alleviate suffering. I'm not saying my thoughts were pure, or that my motives were entirely Christlike, I'm just being honest about how I felt at the time. By the time the devotional was done, I hated every American there. But the real crazy hadn't even started yet.

The missions team staff informed us that the children in the town we were in had no food to eat that day. Most of them ate only once every few days. The information was sobering enough as it was. But then the staff did something that I still consider to be one of the most asinine things I have seen to this day: they brought us lunch.

Lunch. In a building in a town whose children hadn't eaten that day or the day before.

They brought us lunch.

If you ever want to see what James Cammilleri looks like when he's irate, this is one of those moments. "How is this even remotely a missions trip in your minds?" I said. I was irate. "Find me food, and I'll buy it for them."

That's when I wept.

Something inside me broke. Even as I'm typing these words, I'm weeping, and doing so on multiple levels. At that moment, I decided I would never feel sorry for myself again. I wept and repented for a spirit of self-pity that had certainly driven elements of my life. I cried for the missions organization who was probably doing their best to raise awareness about the need in Haiti but who had made fools of themselves by misappropriating resources. And, most of all, I mourned for the 3.2 million children who were without food while someone handed me a sandwich.

"Never again," I remembered saying to myself. "Never again will I be absent from this fight." While Sarah and I couldn't bring relief to all of Haiti's suffering, we could bring healing to one part of their pain.

We would bring them something to eat.

Pay Attention to the Themes of Your Life

One of the most exciting elements of walking with God is becoming aware of the themes of your life. Maybe your profession keeps putting you around people who love medicine. Perhaps you keep getting phone calls to attend certain kinds of conventions, speak to particular groups of people, and come up with solutions for specific types of problems. Or maybe every time you visit a certain side of town, your heart seems to leap out of your chest because of a felt need.

These are what we call themes. They are the reoccurring patterns that keep popping up in time and time again. Most times, you're not even looking for them. They just show up. And it's precisely because we don't look for them that it's even more important we do the hard work of trying to notice them.

If we fail to notice God's themes for our lives, we have a much harder time trying to determine which yes opportunities are from him and which ones aren't. Again, thematic attention is one more way we can know that the next open door is from him and not just random luck. God's next yes for us almost always corresponds to the theme of our lives.

As you can already guess, one of the big themes of our lives was food service. It was something both of us knew from growing up and had found success in as adults. So it shouldn't have been any surprise that God was going to place us in a nation whose needs would resonate with one of our life themes. Food.

Where the Holy Spirit's wisdom comes into play is in determining exactly where your life's themes intersect with felt needs. For example, we could have easily said, "Well, we're good at launching and running successful Burger Kings. Let's open a bunch in Haiti to meet the food need." For many reasons, ranging from economic to cultural, that would have been a bad way to respond to the desperation God was stirring in our hearts. And yet, if a person is not careful, that is precisely the kind of conclusion all of us can jump to in other aspects of our lives. Being good at something does not constitute a theme in and of itself. Instead, we are to look at the heartbeat behind *why* we seem to keep bumping into the same types of people, circumstances, or situations.

While someone on the outside may very well see our success in business and think we are supposed to pick it up and transfer it all to Haiti, this approach would be costly in several critical ways. A far more beneficial critique, however, would be to try and discern why James and Sarah love food service so much. Is it just because they're good at it? Because it's Burger King? Or is it because deep in their hearts, they love serving people and meeting one of the most basic human needs—to eat.

While Burger King may not be transferable to Haiti, making food to eat is. Driving all the activity of our business success, we discovered that God had been telling a story about our lives. He had been weaving the threads together like a master wordsmith eager to release his next volume of work to the world. The story was far less about what kind of restaurant we were operating and far more about why we were longing to rectify hunger. We feed people because we want to be like Jesus.

While there are countless ways to be like Jesus to the world around you, we were becoming his answer to a felt need not only in every town that we ran a restaurant in but also in Haiti. We just didn't know it yet. Remember, knowing God's story for your life is critical to accurately discerning what's of him and what's not.

"I Need Help Feeding Children."

The school and church we ended up building in Passerine were undoubtedly significant if nothing more than for the children who found education in its halls. Despite losing over $7,000 that was supposed to pay contractors and, instead, went into the hands of a corrupt pastor, we still saw the walls raised and the roof put on. Today, that school has over 500 children in elementary and middle school, and they are looking into offering high school academics next.

The real reason we were there had to do with the theme of our lives.

After putting in some long hours of work under the Haitian sun, we sat in a truck with another pastor (along with twelve other people who hung off the vehicle like it was an amusement park ride—such is life in Haiti). Tired, hot, but still desperate to do more, we asked this pastor what he needed, beyond just churches and schools. Little did we know his response would change our lives forever.

"I need help feeding children," he replied.

Both of us sat spellbound in the truck.

I need help feeding children. It was as if God had reached his hand down and smacked us both on the side of our heads. It was one of our lives' themes. We knew how to feed people. Maybe not in Haiti—but we would learn.

The pastor went on to explain how he was receiving aid from the Haitian government and the United States, but that it wasn't actually going to help feed children (which is more common than you might think). He was truly heartbroken and needed some other way to serve starving children.

AT THAT MOMENT, I, James, knew that we were all in. We didn't know what it was yet, but we were going to say yes to something. We were born for this yes.

SEVEN

There's No Such Thing as a Bad Yes

SAYING yes to building the school that cost us an extra $7,000 was a painful experience. But there were some beautiful lessons to be learned.

We were upset with the pastor who stole the money. More to the point, we were both irate. "Don't you understand that you stole from God!" we pleaded with him. But there was no getting through, the money was gone, and the relationship was severed.

That episode was our first real brush with Haitian corruption, and, worse, it was in the one place that it wasn't supposed to be in: the church. In the end, however, God reminded us of two very vital things: (1) It's not our church, it's his, and (2) it's not our money, it's his. After all, the Holy Spirit was the one who prompted us to give in to that particular ministry in that specific town.

But the second lesson was even more critical. It was the lesson of learning to say yes, even when it looked like a bad yes.

We're not sure if you've ever had $7,000 stolen, and then had the person you confront deny it even when you had multiple hard proofs to the contrary. It's frustrating, and feeling taken advantage of can be humiliating. You feel powerless while they appear powerful. We did our best to rest in the idea that everything we had belonged to the Lord, but we couldn't seem to beat the sense that we had said yes to something we shouldn't have.

The lesson learned was this: that saying yes doesn't need to include financial returns. While this may seem rudimentary for some, it was groundbreaking for us. Success in the business world isn't determined by daydreams and wishful thinking. It's determined by profits. And if you don't have profits, you don't have success. Worse still, if you have money stolen from you, you are worse than not successful—you're going out of business. Shutting your doors means your business, and, by some invisible thread of emotional extension, *you* are a failure.

We run into problems when we try and use this basic business logic in the context of kingdom-building. That's because in God's economy, there is no such thing as a bad yes. This is not to say that we should ditch fiscal responsibility in ministry, but it is to say that God's purposes extend beyond the containers we often try to put them in.

In his classic book *Don't Waste Your Sorrows: New Insight Into God's Eternal Purpose for Each Christian in the Midst of Life's*

Greatest Adversities, Paul E. Billheimer explains that nothing is ever wasted in God's kingdom, not even tragedy and loss.[1] Like the apostle Paul wrote, the Holy Spirit will use anything he can to bring good about in the world (Romans 8:28). This is not a license for any thoughtful Christian to go out and misappropriate their power in the name of "God's just gonna use it for good"—that's foolish. But it must cause us to recognize that God will use absolutely anything to showcase his heart for humanity, even if it looks bad at the time. Nothing is ever wasted.

While that building project appeared to be a waste of time and provoked a sense of personal failure, we never would have had the critical conversation with the pastor in the truck about feeding children.

That day, and in the days that followed, we learned that there are no such things as bad yeses for the glory of God. Sure, there might be more efficient, more informed yeses, but there are never inherently bad yeses. What we thought was a bad yes opened exponential doors for us in the years to come. The apparent loss was nothing compared to the gains we would experience. And that is just one example of how the kingdom works. God can take the seemingly impossible, most discouraging situations, and use them for his glory.

Lessons Always Come Back Around

Three years after this first monetary loss, we faced an even more substantial financial setback. Our non-profit organization, Elevating Christian Ministries, was in full swing, and we were doing big things to raise awareness about the needs in Haiti. At one event, we booked one of the nation's most popular worship bands, had keynote speakers, and spent large sums of money to gather the local churches for an unforgettable evening.

The concert itself was powerful and well attended. The feedback was overwhelming, and people were genuinely interested in what God was doing through our work in Haiti. However, due to several factors outside of our control, we ended up losing $30,000 on the event—money that we had hoped would go into equipping the people of Haiti.

It was tempting to wallow in self-pity over the financial loss. What did we do wrong? Maybe we weren't cut out for this. Did we miss you, God? But we had learned this lesson already. In our hearts, we knew what God did with Passerine. He opened doors that no person could shut. So, instead of listening to the voices in the back of our heads, we paid the balance on the event's loss and trusted that God would use it. We chose to believe that there was no such thing as a bad yes from God.

As before, the results exceeded our imaginations. That one event brought us into a relationship with new strategic partners. We garnered favor with leaders in both ministry and business realms. And we had new doors open to serve Haiti that were mind-blowing.

You may be in a place where the obstacles around you seem insurmountable and are downright scary. Maybe you're worried about your next steps failing—your plans crashing down. Perhaps you've even said, "I can't afford to take the next step." We're here to encourage you to be brave.

First, remind yourself that you will have many yeses in your life. Hopefully, you have hundreds and even thousands of yes opportunities that God brings your way. It's critical, however, that you recognize right away that not all of them are going to look good. In fact, some might look really ugly. You'll lose money, time, and even burn a bridge of two. And yet this is a necessary part of your journey.

Getting Out of the Boat

In Matthew 14:22–33, we are told the story of Peter, an ordinary man who walked on water to meet Jesus. Amazingly, Peter manages a few miraculous steps on the sea, defying the laws of physics. But unlike the climactic scene of some Hollywood blockbuster, Peter eventually sinks and has to get rescued by Jesus.

We are so glad Peter failed. No, we're not celebrating his apparent lack of success—but we are appreciative of his humanity. If he had succeeded, Peter would have set the bar very high for the rest of the disciples, and, for that matter, every Christian who would read his story in the years to follow. I'm not sure anyone after him could compare. Do you have any friends or family who've walked on water?

But there is more to it than that.

First of all, notice that Peter didn't refuse Jesus's summons.

He said yes when confronted with a physically impossible request. Look at these verses:

> *28 "Lord, if it's you," Peter replied, "tell me to come to you on the water."*
> *29 "Come," he said.*
> *Then Peter got down out of the boat, walked on the water, and came toward Jesus.*

This is far from a failure. Somebody needs to throw that dude a party! Think about it—when confronted with a humanly impossible situation, Peter's response was not, "Um, Jesus. Do you know anything about the law of gravity and the surface tension of water? This isn't going to end well. I've been a fisherman for a long time, and, well, when we get out of a boat in the middle of the sea, we sink 100% of the time."

Instead, the scripture says, "Then Peter got out of the boat." Who does that? This is astounding faith. But more importantly, this is evidence of absolute trust in and sold-out love for Jesus.

One of the biggest head games we play with ourselves as Christians is trying to determine whether or not we can trust what we're hearing, and, by extension, trust God. After all, has anyone seen him appear in clouds and fire lately? Do you or someone you know hear his audible voice on a daily basis? This is not to say such things can't or don't happen, but by and large, this is not the experience of the Christian majority. Instead, we have leadings, impressions, a still small voice, and fortuitous accidents that are much too detailed to be mere coincidences. And when those things line up and are accompanied by the sense of God's presence, we know something big is about to happen. But the question remains, do we trust him?

For Peter, the answer was yes. So he got out of the boat. He said yes to the opportunity.

Secondly, notice that God was calling Peter in the context of a theme in a disciple's life—being on the water. Remember, Peter was a career fisherman and the oldest of all the disciples. He'd spent a lot of time on the water. While we might be inferring a little too much into the text here, we actually believe that something about this crazy invitation made sense to Peter. He knew the sea. He knew fishing boats. And he knew Jesus. This was all familiar territory. Jesus was simply giving him the next piece of the puzzle. "It's time to get out of your comfort zone, Peter," Jesus said. "You know this place. It's part of the theme of your life. But now we're gonna try something nuts. You ready?"

Maybe, if Jesus had Peter on top of some ancient construction crane and asked him to step off the end, Peter wouldn't have said yes. He hadn't grown up on a crane. He couldn't handle heights. Instead, Jesus was offering the next step of faith in the context of Peter's ordinary world.

In the same way, God tends to offer us yes invitations in the context of our life's varied themes. Contrary to what some people might assume, Peter wasn't operating in blind faith. As such, God rarely asks us to leap blind. Instead, he prompts us to move into what presents itself as the next viable faith-step that makes sense with where we've been and where we're headed. For Peter, that was saying yes in a fishing boat during a storm. For you, it could be saying yes to help an employee, take a trip with a family member, give someone a car, mow someone's lawn, or start a new business. Yeses are everywhere, but learning to trust the Holy Spirit as he prompts us to act tends to work in conjunction with the themes of our lives.

Let's look at Peter's story for one more lesson that pertains to the idea of there being no such thing as bad yeses from God. Look at this next verse:

> *30 But when he saw the wind, he was afraid and, beginning to sink, cried out, "Lord, save me!"*

It would be easy to assume that Peter failed at this moment. You're supposed to be walking on water, but instead, you're sinking. We can hear the conversations now as Jesus helped Peter back on the boat.

"Way to go, Pete," Thomas said with a sarcastic tone. "Real nice job out there."

"Find any fish while you were underwater?" Matthew asked.

"Nay," Judas added. "He was too busy letting Jesus down."

What we find interesting is that, at the end of the story, Jesus doesn't necessarily admonish Peter for sinking. He rebukes him for something totally different:

> *31 Immediately Jesus reached out his hand and caught him. "You of little faith," he said, "why did you doubt?"*

What Jesus was responding to was Peter's cry for help. Said another way, when Peter said, "Lord, save me!" it was because he thought maybe Jesus wouldn't unless he asked.

If we sink while saying yes, that is never the thing that invites God's examination. To sink is human. But when we fail to trust that he will rescue us? That is what caused Jesus to rebuke Peter. God can do a lot with a sinking person but very little with someone who won't trust him.

When you say that everything in your life belongs to God, it also means that you relinquish your ideas about how God will use you. It doesn't mean some ideas or themes won't come back around, but it does mean you are open to whatever possibilities the Holy Spirit has for you—even the ones you don't see yet. We highly doubt Peter woke up that morning and knew he was going to be presented with a significant test. But he learned a valuable lesson that day, even in the midst of an apparent "bad yes."

Peter would go on to have several other bad yes moments in his life, some embarrassing, others downright disgraceful. But, in the kingdom, nothing is ever lost. All of those apparent bad yes decisions eventually led to Peter being one of the most outspoken ministers of his generation, and one of the first leaders in what we know today as the Christian church. Scripture records Peter as being the first to preach a Gospel message following the events surrounding Pentecost in Acts

2:14–42. What was it that turned this water-sinking, mouthy betrayer into a passionate public preacher? Among many other reasons, we believe it was because he continued to say yes to Jesus despite his apparent failures.

WE WANT to challenge you not to hold back from God, not even a little. Be all in when you say yes—hand over everything you have and submit to him. Remember, you can trust him to rescue you even if you start to sink because it's never the sinking that concerns him.

And it can't be a grudging yes, either. None of us are fooling God. Our hearts determine the quality of the yes. Remember, it's human nature to make the yes deceitful or half-hearted, but it's Christ's nature in us to make it genuine. When you're responding to the Holy Spirit with a pure heart, it's impossible to fail him. When your heart is perpetually positioned to "bless and do not curse" (Roms 12:14), there is truly no end to how God will use you. As for the pastor who stole the money, we determined not to let other people's failures preclude our obedience. We are responsible for what God tells us to do, not what others do with what we've given them.

EIGHT

Building Greatness Out of Yeses

WHEN SOMEONE STOLE FROM US, our response was to give more.

Hold on. You wanna run that by us again?

Sure. That pastor stole thousands of dollars from us that should have been going to a building project and feeding kids. And when we had the opportunity, we gave to that ministry even more than we'd lost.

You'd better explain that for me.

Gladly.

People have debated the meaning of Jesus's "turn the other cheek" teaching in Matthew 5:38–40 for as long as the New Testament has been around. If you're unfamiliar with it, we encourage you to jump on your Bible app now and read through it. It's a very challenging passage by anyone's standards, and people are masters at taming it to suit their agendas whenever they get uncomfortable with it.

In our younger years, this scripture would have been a pain in our butts—to put it gently. Young James would have dropped you if you crossed him, and young Sarah would have dismissed you before you even got close. But when Jesus gets ahold of anyone's heart, and that person starts to discover the life-changing principles that drive the upside-down kingdom of God, a "turn the other cheek" teaching is no longer a hardship—it's an invitation to greatness.

It wasn't enough for us to walk away from that deceptive pastor in Passerine. We felt that if we let his insincere actions overcome us, it would only jade us toward a nation we knew God was calling us to serve. Besides, we wondered if the theft itself wasn't another yes opportunity. Little did we know, the investment would usher us toward our most significant work ever.

Rather than burn bridges, we decided to continue to invest in that ministry despite our flesh's desire to punch someone's face in. (*That was James's line, not mine.* —Sarah). Granted, we weren't about to entrust more money to someone who had proven they were unable to handle it. That would have been unwise on several levels. However, we still believed in the ministry's work to feed and educate children. So we found other trustworthy channels to invest through and gave another $40,000. (*But I still wanted to punch someone's face in.* —James). We fed 1,000 children for two years with that organization, and we felt God smile.

Something was being birthed in our hearts—something big.

Working in Passerine taught us another valuable lesson. We learned to look at the mission and not the man. As we already mentioned (and James not-so-subtly alluded to), it would have been easy for us to react out of anger. Instead, we realized that we couldn't afford to let stupid people sidetrack us from what God had called us to do. And neither can you.

Very often, good people get sidelined because they get sidetracked. They start doing things they're not good at or have no natural gifts for, or they engage in behavior that isn't genuinely Christlike, all because they are unable to properly manage their flesh and stay focused. This simple thought of resisting the urge to get distracted has helped us navigate many troubling situations that could have very quickly ended our ministry in Haiti and bankrupt some or all of our businesses in the United States. Instead, we chose to take the low road—which is actually the high road—and bless the ministry despite how people had misused the money. The broader vision of their ministry, and ours, was at stake, and we were not about to be the ones who shipwrecked the task of feeding children on the dumb decisions of severely misguided adults.

The Best Big Things Start Small

One of the most beautiful things about working to expand the kingdom of God is that we Christians rarely know what we're doing at the time. We don't see the front side of the tapestry.

Instead, we've got our heads down on the backside of the art, trying to pull threads through, and hope whoever's directing the process knows what they're doing.

Many times, that's exactly how we felt in Haiti. Heads down, get the job done. After all, kids' lives are literally on the line. There's no room to mamby-pamby around.

Getting involved with ministries that wanted to feed children was one of the most life-giving things we had ever done together. And even when it sucked, we still felt God was breathing on it. But serving kids food also presented a slew of new challenges. Rather than see them as setbacks, we saw them as obstacles to a goal—and nothing was going to stop us.

The first thing we did was state the big picture. *We are here to feed children.* We weren't feeling called to rebuild the capital building, restore oceanfront properties, reform the education system, or overhaul healthcare. No. We wanted to see kids in one village have something to eat, every day, and find nourishment for their little bodies. That was it. It wasn't a "ministry" that needed a non-profit entity to house it. It didn't have a logo, staff, or operating budget. It was just us saying, "We've got to do something."

The second thing we learned was that we were not going to trust "just any" Haitians with money. Their entire worldview differed so much from ours concerning money that what we considered sin was acceptable for them. This is not to throw anyone under the bus. It is meant to recognize that their ways of handling money were incompatible with our goal of getting children fed. Additionally, we were not saying that helping educate people in money management wasn't a worthwhile task. It just wasn't our goal. We were working to avoid distractions wherever we could. Part of saying yes is identifying and safeguarding your path from everyone else's noes. This is also known as *wisdom*.

Third, we faced economic and agricultural problems. What we were looking to do was no small thing, even for one little village. It wasn't like running a food pantry in a US city where you could strike deals with local food distributors and get the tractor-trailers to unload extra items as a hub. No way. In the village we were trying to feed kids in, there was nothing.

We'll repeat it in case we weren't clear.

There. Was. Nothing.

If we wanted it, we had to go somewhere else to find it, which included the raw ingredients to make these kids something to eat. And that was harder than it looked.

In the 1990s, then-President Bill Clinton proposed and passed legislation to subsidize rice production for Haiti by growing it in the United States and shipping it south.[1] Three years after the 7.0-magnitude earthquake rocked the island nation, Clinton said he had struck a "devil's bargain," one that "may have been good for some of my farmers in Arkansas, but it has not worked" for the people of Haiti.[2] Worse still, not only did the US's agricultural position increase food costs for the people, but it took farming jobs away from the Haitian nationals. And what rice Haitians do grow—brown rice with far more nutrients—is twice as expensive as the American rice. So, to feed a child American rice and beans in 2015 would have cost us $1 per day, with the majority of those funds going right back to the United States.

The more we learned, the more our stomachs turned in knots.

Eventually, it dawned on us that we needed to think outside the box. The only reason we were thinking about serving the kids rice was because "that's what Haitians eat." And while there's certainly an argument for observing cultural norms, we were talking about children starving to death right in front of our eyes. There was no media coverage. No nightly special. FEMA wasn't there, and few if any American churches had been this far out. We were it.

"So we're gonna feed them wheat," James said. I realized that wheat had far more nutrients in it than rice, and we could get it cheap. But right away, I had people refute the idea.

"But Haitians don't eat bread," people said.

My response?

"I don't care! If they want to eat, they'll eat bread." And that was that.

In the pursuit of your yes, recognize that well-meaning people can be used by the enemy to interfere with God's plans. This does not mean we don't listen to wise counsel when it comes. But we must pay attention to people and ideas that might delay or even thwart necessary actions in the name of self-gratification (theirs, not yours). If someone's "bright idea" threatens to hinder progress and resists life, then it's most likely not from the Holy Spirit. Instead, kingdom ideas always rise above human norms in the pursuit of life—*and* life abundant (John 10:10). Show us the quest for life, and we'll show you Jesus.

Now that we were on our way to sourcing wheat, we needed a way to bake bread. For that, we turned to a family member back in the states who came up with a design for an oven with components that could be sourced and assembled in Haiti. It was a simple, fool-proof design, and we loved it. It was time to make bread.

When God Multiplies Stuff, Look Out

By April of the following year, we were back in Haiti, and we were on a mission. We carried in 100 pounds of wheat and ten burners, intending to build four bread ovens in four days. There was no plan to start a ministry; we were just saying yes to come back and feed kids. Months of planning, negotiating, and preparation came down to that day, and we wanted to get it right.

As we recalled our first "missions trip" from the year before, we remembered watching the Americans do all the work for various projects around the villages while the Haitians stood around and did nothing. Something about that was all wrong to us. While it appeared to be a gesture of goodwill, we soon realized that those kinds of trips weren't helping Haiti—they were hurting it. The United States had already proven that providing Haiti deliverables that they did not labor for themselves was a disaster. It removed many intangible things that any healthy person and community need to survive, including self-respect, self-reliance, and the dignity that comes from making your own way in the world.

Instead, Haiti has rotted from the inside out, suffering under constant handouts and free labor from other countries. The American missionary trips were not empowering Haitians to build their way out of the pit they were in. Instead, they were perpetuating captivity by enabling Haitians to continue to live at the bottom. Meanwhile, back home, American churches were celebrating advances made by their teams in erecting walls or digging ditches.

We decided Haitians would build their bread ovens. We would be there to guide, troubleshoot, and support. But we made it clear: this wasn't our gig. It was theirs.

Little did we know at the time, but promoting Haitians to do their own work would become a hallmark of our quiet gift to them. The goal wasn't to be their savior. That position was already filled. The goal was to feed them until they could feed themselves.

And for those Americans who wanted to partner with us? We wouldn't let them lift a finger. Instead, our goal was to expose them to poverty, give them opportunities to have their hearts break for hurting people, and encourage them to grow closer to God. But it was God's job to change their hearts, not ours, just as it was the locals' job to build the ovens, not ours.

We succeeded in seeing those four ovens built in four days, and to the nay-sayers' chagrin, the children loved the bread muffins we made them. So much so that before long, we ran out of wheat. We hadn't planned on the ovens and the bread being such a success! So we scrambled for the next best resource we could find: cornmeal. It wasn't as nutritious as wheat, but it was better for the kids than rice, so we made do.

Giving Haitians responsibility for production went far beyond merely building bread ovens. Someone had to keep these fires going, and we knew that must fall on them too. We remain convinced that building indigenous businesses, owned and operated by Haitian nationals, is one of the many ways that Haiti will not only hoist itself out of the pit, but it's how they will keep themselves from sliding back in.

NINE

Secrets to Growing Strong Yeses

"I'M GOING to have you finish what other Christians started."

This phrase is what we sensed the Holy Spirit saying to us in August of 2016 when we arrived in Pelige, Haiti. We were in the middle of building more bread ovens to feed children when God sidetracked us, opening the door to visit another church and school in the area.

To our amazement, the congregation had been meeting in structures not even half-complete and prone to weather damage. The roof was at risk of collapsing, the benches were falling apart, and the floor wasn't suitable for foot traffic. When we asked about the condition of the buildings, we were surprised to hear that missionaries had started the building campaign but were unable to finish. Without other options, the congregation was forced to continue using the space despite its condition.

When we looked at the property, we knew right away it was something we could complete—and quickly. Again, we told Jesus that we didn't want him to have to ask someone else to do the work. "Let your eyes stop on us," we said. Just as before, we activated the local community to engage in the labor and then watched as a half-built church and school were brought to completion.

The story reminded us of two precious lessons, one hopeful and one cautionary.

In Paul's first letter to the Corinthian churches, he reminds us that when it comes to doing the work of the ministry, one person plants a seed and a different person waters it, but it's God who causes it to grow (1 Corinthians 3:6-8). Meaning, we can never be too sure what part we are playing in someone else's journey, but in the end, it is God who is orchestrating it all for his glory.

It's often easy to point fingers at successful pastors, evangelists, or worship leaders and grow "righteously jealous" of the harvest they seem to bring in with their messages and songs so easily. In reality, however, every person those leaders minister to has probably already been ministered to by a family member, a next-door neighbor, or a co-worker. As members of the body of Christ, we have the unique honor of playing our specific role in co-laboring with God and building his kingdom together. As a result, we never can be too sure of what part we're playing. Our task is to say yes and be faithful to the opportunities he brings our way.

The second lesson we learned in Pelige was about

finishing what you start. While we may never know the reasons those missionaries abandoned their project mid-swing, we saw the emotional effects and the physical dangers it placed on a needy congregation. The pitiful state of those structures reinforced in us the conviction that we must finish what we start. This is a critical part of what faithfulness is. And even if you can't finish a project yourself, you do your very best to arrange for others to complete what you began. Your next yes may very well hinge on a past yes's pending completion.

There is one more note to make about our time in Pelige—an unusual but very telling postscript. Every time the pastor preached, a large pillar stood directly between him and the congregation. The support was needed, of course, so that the unfinished roof didn't collapse. But after we installed proper trussing, we were able to remove the column. The pastor and the congregation could finally see one another, and the physical barrier that represented a half-built yes had been taken away with a fully built yes.

Lessons in Rice Country

Our frustration with mismanagement didn't end in Pelige.

One might easily argue that Haiti is a master class in mismanagement, especially when it comes to money. Part of our ministry today is teaching people how to wisely steward money using Biblical principles as a pathway to deeper understanding and financial freedom. But in October of 2016, we were headed to the most impoverished place we'd seen anywhere on earth.

We left Gonaives, headed east, and plunged deep into the heart of rice country. Three hours later, we arrived at Drouin, a place where the sewers and the streets were indistinguishable. The sheer poverty of the landscape was second only to the overwhelming odor that permeated the air and filled every breath we took. The people were so poor and the economy so backward that the workers couldn't even afford to eat the rice they grew. Thus we came to understand why people had told us, "There's poor, and then there's Drouin."

But we felt that God had yes opportunities for us in this village too. And so we started work on a church, a school, and bread ovens for the local community. Unfortunately, the conditions were so adverse that eventually even the Haitian workers had to abandon their job sites. For us, there was no going back. As we saw in Pelige, we weren't going to leave a project half-baked. We'd see what others had done, and we refused to do the same. "We're here to serve," we said. "And we won't quit."

We popped enough chlorine tabs in our water to kill the bubonic plague and then set to work. If Drouin was another yes opportunity, we weren't going to let the Lord down, nor those beautiful people. We labored among them to finish the projects we said we would. Today, the school has over 150 children, all of whom receive bread daily, and a staff of paid teachers on our payroll.

When God brings you a yes, treat it like your most precious

opportunity, because to someone around you, it may very well be the difference between life and death.

The Beauty of Getting Organized

By the time 2017 rolled around, our work in Haiti had grown to such a degree that we needed to form a non-profit organization to help manage the activity. We were learning how to listen to the voice of the Holy Spirit in each town we visited and assess the needs of each community he sent us to partner with. We also continued to recognize the importance of finishing what we started and serving people even when others were running away. Advancing any worthwhile goal takes a certain tenacity that separates you from the rest of the pack, one that says, "We are here, we are not going anywhere, and we mean business."

But with all the success came new challenges. We couldn't maintain our pace without restructuring, and we weren't sure how to formalize ourselves or even what we should do with all the businesses we were already running aside from our expanding work in Haiti. Then came a very critical moment where we thought of selling our businesses solely to focus on missions work.

If there was a piece of advice this book could provide those who are experiencing the pressures of growth, it is this: seek wise counsel from those with long track records of success. It's often easier to read a line like that in a book than it is to actuate it. Sometimes we don't have access to high-caliber individuals, and connecting with them might take time, money, and tenacity. But in the end, God can use one key piece of advice to change your life radically.

For us, a critical turning point came from a word given to us by a pastor of a two-hundred-year-old church in northern New York, Kirk Gilchrist. Not only had Kirk been pastoring successfully for several decades, but he'd also owned and operated several different companies that gave away millions of dollars in profits.

In light of all the significant work we were doing in Haiti, we told Kirk that flipping burgers with Burger King just wasn't cutting it. Our sincere enthusiasm for "full time" ministry, as we called it, was far more enticing than managing restaurants. But Kirk lovingly challenged us to reconsider.

"You're called to do both, guys," he said. "God's clearly blessing you to operate in the business and ministry worlds. Why abandon one for the other when you can do both?"

That thought had never dawned on us before, at least not the way that Kirk presented. But the anointing on his life for both business and ministry had a way of shining a light on the anointing of our lives to do the same. That one crucial conversation had a dramatic impact on our decision to move forward with a foot in both worlds. We shudder to think what would have happened had we not sought Kirk's counsel when we did. God was indeed watching out for us.

Soon after, Elevating Christian Ministries was born, incorporated out of a desire to see Haiti raised from the mire of natural, economic, and political tragedy and walk in the abundant life Christ came to give humanity. In just a few short months, we had fed and educated hundreds of children, employed teachers and entrepreneurs, and gotten a glimpse of what life could look like in a devastated land. Now, with ECM, we were able to formalize the work God was calling us to.

The Holy Spirit was not only forming us organizationally but also relationally. Just as we had learned the power of building proper teams in the foodservice industry, so too were we discovering the value of having the right people around us on the ground in Haiti. Fewer things highlighted this more than when we brought our friend Mike Shipman on board ECM.

Mike's pastoral heart turned out to be just what the ministry needed at the time. His many years as a pastor in various cities allowed him to be conversant with a wide range of people.

We, James and Sarah, came from a position of making money. It's what we knew. But most of the pastors we met in Haiti came from a place of asking for money. This juxtaposition can often be brutal, and it's easy for misunderstandings to turn heated and bridges to get burned.

During one trip in particular, Mike accompanied us to meet a pastor in significant need of materials and funds to care for his congregation. The pastor had been praying for fourteen years for God to send someone to his remote village, so you can imagine his excitement when some crazy white Americans arrived. But where we were ready to do something practical—to roll up our sleeves, buy materials, and higher contractors—Mike took a much different and astonishing route.

He offered to pray with the pastor.

This provision of prayer caught us completely off guard, not because it wasn't right—if anything, it was amazing! We quickly recognized that God was once again bringing people into our lives whose giftedness complemented our own. Where we were ready to jump in and start building stuff, Mike recognized the pastor's heart's need and offered to pray before doing anything else.

Mike's prayer not only included wisdom and discernment for what ECM might be able to do, but comfort and strength for the pastor as he engaged in God's kingdom-building work. When it was over, we realized that the Holy Spirit had just breathed on the moment and, more importantly, that he had blown on our team.

As we'll discuss more, having God strengthen your team by adding people to it is one of the greatest blessings you can ever walk in. Strength doesn't just come from numbers. Strength also comes from people who show up at the right times. Whether that's a word spoken in season, like Kirk's, or a staff member helping bridge gaps and complement your skill sets, like Mike, paying attention to and learning to cherish key partnerships is essential to leveraging the most out of each yes opportunity God gives you.

TEN

Empowering Others to Discover Their Yeses

AS CHRIST MATURES and moves us forward in life, one of the most beautiful gifts is being able to help other people discover their own yes invitations from heaven. While we could cite countless examples of how this is our business work, including the joy we have of empowering hundreds of employees and business partners to uncover their next steps in life, we'd like to stay focused on Haiti. Beyond raising awareness about the plight of those facing significant hardship, using Haiti as an example allows us to point out important aspects of the right ways to empower others as well as the wrong ways.

Investing Without Harming

As ECM continued to grow, serving more children, building more bread ovens, and raising more funds to build churches and schools, we became acutely aware of a potential problem with our presence. We found ourselves riding a line as foreigners, one that risked inadvertently hurting people when all we wanted to do was help.

In the classic modernist perspective of Christian missions work, affluent Christ-centered nations or populations view those in economic need as the aim of their charity. This is mostly and rightly driven by the writer James's admonition "to look after orphans and widows in their distress" (James 1:27). In an era when being a widow meant you had no income, and being an orphan meant you'd most likely never see adulthood, James challenged Christians to care for the economically oppressed. This notion is then intrinsically coupled with Jesus's closing remarks, commonly referred to as the Great Commission, found in Mark's Gospel: "Go into all the world and preach the gospel to all creation" (Mark 16:15). The combined result of these two passages is what we might call the Über Great Commission that has driven much of the church's activities: to send out missionaries and care for the poor.

Many other poignant books have been written on the inherent pitfalls of affluent societies attending to the needs of impoverished people groups. This is not to say that such work shouldn't be undertaken—far from it. But those providing aid must be aware of the impact that their presence has and to examine ways to mitigate their work's unhealthy side effects. For example, in their book *When Helping Hurts*, authors Steve Corbett and Brian Fikkert illustrate the putative physiological effects that the poor suffer when they are not a part of their own transformation.[1] And as Robert D. Lupton points out, quick and easy acts of charity often do more to give the donor a good feeling than assisting the poor in climbing out of cycles of destitution.[2] Rather, it is when charity and creative entrepreneurial problem solving come together, taking into account the dignity of those in need, that we can discover surer ways forward than fleeting handouts.[3]

As previously discussed, we encountered the adverse effects of long-distance charity early on in our trips to Haiti. Whether in the form of government handouts and agricultural subsidies or in church missions work that disempowered Haitians for engaging in their own processes of liberation, we didn't need to look far to see how giving can hurt those you're trying to help if not done carefully.

We wouldn't learn about resources like the books mentioned above until much later in our work. But fortunately for us, our years in food service provided a deep understanding of and value for the ethics of hard work, personal accountability, and the irreplaceable dignity that comes from taking responsibility for one's self. More than a handout, the people we met in Haiti needed these values—they were starving not just for food but for validation of their right to exist and contribute to the world. This is what ECM wanted to help provide.

We'd seen firsthand how monetary gifts were misused. The $7,000 theft in Passerine wasn't the only time money had been misappropriated. Such instances were incredible teachers and highlighted just how vital stewardship and money management really was. The real reason $7,000 was misused was that no one ever taught that pastor how to care for $7.00. So when outside organizations—for churches and nonprofits to government agencies and companies—send money without education, people suffer. But even something as innocent as volunteering to paint a wall as a foreigner instead of handing the paintbrush to a Haitian in need of work adversely affects the economy.

We decided early on that ECM would teach Haitian nationals how to create wealth for themselves, their families, and their communities. We didn't want to westernize them. Instead, we wanted to give them something handouts could never provide: skills. Teaching skills is messy work. It's hard, and it requires lots of patience and face time. It often ends in disaster, as not everyone wants to learn. But in the end, we were convinced that it was one of the non-negotiable essentials in seeing Haiti lifted from the mire.

We Bring This, You Bring That

One of the stories that best illustrates the collaborative nature of ECM's ministry approach comes from our time in a community in Haiti's lower western-reaching peninsula. Before the 2010 earthquake, La Source was a vibrant village, boasting fisheries, crops, and over 500 in their school. But when tragedy struck, the community lost something many of us take for granted—their water supply. The once productive and self-sustaining town was crippled and unable to recover.

When we met with La Source's leaders, the first thing we did was ask them for their ideas on how they could bring their town back to life. One of the tragedies that many well-meaning do-gooders often perpetuate is omitting this necessary step of inviting the subject of their charity to the whiteboard sessions. After we posed the initial questions, we got out of the way entirely. Seeing people dream about the possibilities of what their town could be as seen from their eyes, not ours, was a wonderful thing.

After everything was discussed, it was determined that one of the most expedient ways to restore health to the town was providing access to a freshwater well 250-feet from the village. While the water supply was healthy, the town leaders lacked the necessary equipment to reach it and bring the water to the town. So they turned to us as asked for assistance. But rather than swoop in and provide all the monies, resources, and labor, we knew that activating the town's leadership was just as important as mining the well for water.

"We will take care of the pump and the solar panel to run it," we said. "But you have to provide the wiring, the waterline, and the labor to install it." And with that, our collaborative project was underway.

It was exciting to watch a village, one fueled by hope, engage in their own revitalization over something as simple as a hose and some copper wire. But before long, they had the materials and provided ample labor to erect the equipment and run the waterline to the town's center. Where water had been scarce for years, suddenly it was overflowing—literally.

THIS ISN'T JUST a story about activating Haitians to reclaim a previously inaccessible well. This is a lesson in the value of trusting other people with their own destiny and inspiring them to discover their own yes invitations.

"Helicopter parenting" is when a child's father, mother, or guardian swoops in and tries to alleviate their pain, difficulty, or trial at the first sign of struggle. Surely, delivering a child from any real peril is of paramount responsibility. But when a young person has the ability to work out their own problems and discern a way forward, even if they lack the means, a parent must resist the urge to step in. If they don't, they risk raising a person who, in adulthood, is unfit for the demands and pressures of life.

Likewise, when we encounter anyone in need, whether familial or otherwise, our most significant help is not in solving all their problems. Instead, we are called to be present and, when appropriate, ask questions that have the potential to help *them* to unlock their own way forward. Sometimes, that is our only role—but what a role! There are few joys greater than witnessing another human being recognize yes invitations. When the lights come on—when the proverbial or literal well is discovered just 250-feet from the village—look out. More often than not, all people need is a little push and a nudge of encouragement, and they'll do the rest if they're hungry enough.

Another problem with helicopter parenting is that the parent is inevitably trying to assert their way of doing things on the child. Such behavior effectively robs the child of self-discovery and, potentially, of finding a better way to overcome the problem. (Children growing up to be better than their parents—imagine that). In the same way, had we told the people of La Source our American way of sourcing water, we would have not only robbed them of their own creativity, but we would have never even learned about the well. In reality, we would have been too busy trying to discover water somewhere else. Our job was not to superimpose our cultural norms on them; our job was to help activate their inherent ingenuity with complimentary effort.

In the Gospel of John, Jesus has an unusual encounter with a lame man (John 5:1–9). For thirty-eight years, the crippled man was unable to walk and was forced to beg for his livelihood. When Jesus came along, he asked the man if he wanted to be healed, to which the man replied that he did but lacked the resources. Upon hearing this, Jesus seemingly granted the man's desperate hope but delivered the news in a strange way.

"Get up," Jesus exclaimed. "Pick up your mat and walk!"

This powerful encounter highlights one of many fascinating aspects about God's healing power in our lives: that he often works collaboratively with us. Meaning, he invites us, the person being healed, to join in and be responsive to the work he is doing. Think of it this way: Jesus had enough power to make the man levitate and stand up if he wanted. Instead, Jesus's instructions were for the man to enter into belief by doing something he hadn't done in thirty-eight years —to stand up on his own.

Reading that story 2,000 years removed from its place in history has a way of stripping the potency from the scene. Added to it is the fact that the story is "in the Bible," which can make it feel "oh, so holy." While scripture is undoubtedly holy, and the Bible is nothing to scoff at, we must not allow our religious assumptions to rob the narrative of its power. The fact is, most of us probably would have been shocked at the way Jesus handled this healing. Had we been with him walking down the street, I imagine some of us would have been offended at how Jesus spoke to an invalid on the corner. Just imagine a homeless person holding a cardboard sign hunkered down on a sidewalk. How dare Jesus demean the man by ordering him to do the very thing he cannot do! Is Jesus that insensitive? Does he lack that much decorum?

But Jesus knew exactly what he was doing. "Of course he did," someone might say. "He was God incarnate." Yes, but he was also acutely aware of how we humans are wired. He understood then what he still knows today: that the highest level of growth we achieve is that which we are invited into and take on for ourselves. Ask anyone who has ever been through a trial, and they will tell you the same thing. We don't grow in the valleys. We grow in the struggle.

The mission of those with resources is not to heap them on others in need and then walk away, trusting them to figure life out. We have learned that bringing lasting help entails less giving of stuff and more giving of time. This could be time for a phone call to hear someone out. This might be a series of emails to be a sounding board for someone's idea. Or this might be a trip to meet face to face to have them show you their vision. Either way, the point is that helping people see the yeses right in front of them is much more a journey of discovery than it is an economic exchange of goods and services. Look for ways to work together, ask questions that stimulate development, and then provide the resources that constitute your part of the equation.

ELEVEN

When Yes Feels Too Heavy

(COMBATTING THE "YES FATIGUE" MYTH)

WHEN PEOPLE SEE all that we do and learn about all that we've been through, they sometimes ask the question: "That's great, but isn't it tiring?" Or, said another way, "Can't you say yes one too many times?" More often than not, these questions are coming from people who are burnt out and tired from attempting to live a yes-life. But as you've likely already concluded, they are missing some key ingredients to what yes-living looks like.

These well-meaning skeptics aren't alone in their wondering, either. Perhaps even you are thinking, "James and Sarah, that's awesome. But I've said yes to stuff, and it has cost me a lot—more than I was able to afford. And now look at me. I don't even know if I can hear the voice of God anymore." Would it surprise you to know that we've been there too?

The Fool's Art of Telling God What to Do

By the time April of 2017 rolled around, I, James, was shaking a fist at heaven, saying, "I'm done building churches, and you can't make me!" I was tired of helping town after town, pastor after pastor, building churches, schools, and bread ovens. It was hot, tiring work, and I was continuously dealing with unscrupulous characters—many of whom were brothers and sisters in Christ.

And yet there I was, telling God what he could and couldn't do. Perhaps it was the hot Haitian sun bringing back some of the old James. Or maybe I had finally overextended myself, and this was the end of our ministry in Haiti. Either way, I was frustrated with God, and with myself.

SAYING yes isn't always easy, but it is still right.

We're going to say that again in a different way so that it has a better chance of sinking in. Saying yes to God doesn't guarantee that the path will be smooth, but it is sure to be the right thing for you to do at the right time. Responding to an invitation from the Holy Spirit is always the best move to make.

As we've already discussed, the closer we move toward the Father's heart, the easier it is for us to make out his heartbeat. Thus, we can learn to sense which opportunities are from him and which ones aren't as a matter of instinct. Jesus even said that "my sheep listen to my voice; I know them, and they follow me" (John 10:27). There is a very real sense that as we fly close to the Good Shepherd, we learn his mannerisms, the tones of his voice, and the cadence of his speech. This doesn't make following through on certain yeses less challenging, but it does give us reassurance that God is genuinely behind everything that's going on. In other words, knowing that God spoke something is the ultimate hedge against hopelessness.

So you've said yes to God, and suddenly you find yourself in a pickle. The big question becomes, "Now what?" And then, in extreme cases, we throw our hands up in the air, telling God what he can and can't do. For us, this happened while trying to cope with a rapidly expanding ministry in a deeply needy nation. For you, it might be a relationship entering into an uncharted phase, a new business venture gone sideways, or a move to a location you thought was going to be flowing with proverbial milk and honey but, instead, brought you a whole lot of hurt.

"How can this possibly be God's will for my life?" we ask. "Did he miss the memo somehow? Because this *sucks*."

But as we've already noted, we don't grow in the sweet sunshine filled valleys of life. We grow where the air is thin, the temperature is cold, and the company is lonely. We grow on the mountaintop.

It's also on this mountaintop where we have the opportunity—yes, another one—to discover an incredible principle of

God's kingdom. Paul referred to it best when he said, "When I am weak, then I am strong" (2 Corinthians 12:10). At first glance, this oxymoron seems to be the rambling of a lunatic or at least some sort of mistranslation of the original text. "How can a person be strong when they are weak?" Fortunately, Paul goes on to explain that when our energies seem insufficient for the tasks that God has brought our way, the Holy Spirit has a supernatural way of showing up to compensate for our lack. This is the true principle of partnership. Not only do we need earthly partners in the journey, but we need the greatest co-laborer of all: Christ. Paul even said that the Holy Spirit's words to him were "my power is made perfect in weakness." In other words, our weakness becomes an invitation for the divine to show up. We *want* to be tired as his strength is going to be so relevant in our lives.

IT'S critical to note that his strength isn't some "nice idea" that floats around while we're wasting away in our toil. Instead, his power is *more* real than fatigue ever could be—to the point that if we're tired from doing things that he's called us into, it's proof that we're relying on something other than his presence to keep us afloat. Weariness amid well-doing is not evidence of heaven's absence but of our resistance to doing things God's way. In other words, if you're not relying on him to get things done, you're going to get tired out. For me, James, I was so self-motivated that I had to go to the bottom to learn how to rely on Jesus. There was no other way out than through the basement. That kind of logic doesn't make sense to the world, but it makes perfect sense in the kingdom.

When Flesh Gets in the Way

We've never met anyone who got tired because they said yes to God, but we've met plenty of people who are tired because they said yes to people. That's a bold statement, we know. And we risk getting a lot of people mad at us for it too. After all, aren't pastors and missionaries and Christian therapists endlessly tired from all the work they do for God? While we don't doubt anyone's motives or the quality of their character, unless they give us reason to, we believe it's critical to discern the difference between doing things for Jesus and doing things for people. The line between the two can often become blurry, especially as we spend more and more time in territory we were never meant to live in.

As the old parable goes about the frog in the pot of warm water, a potentially disastrous situation doesn't feel that bad at first. It's often hard to distinguish between doing things for others because it's right on the one hand, and the feel-good effects we get from doing those things on the other. Our actions can even unwittingly feed secret fears of letting others down or cause us to push ourselves because we need to meet the expectations of those we admire. Eventually, the frog realizes something's gone horribly wrong and that they've been duped into thinking this wasn't all about taking a nice warm bath but, instead, getting served up as *Grenouille*.

Aside from trying to do everything ourselves—apart from God's strength intervening in our weaknesses—one of the biggest mistakes we can make as Christians is trying to please people. For more on this subject, we recommend Melody Beattie's *Codependent No More: How to Stop Controlling Others and Start Caring for Yourself,* and Henry Cloud and John Townsend's *Boundaries: When to Say Yes, How to Say No to Take Control of Your Life, which both* serve as robust benchmarks on how to live free from the constraints of other people's wills and expectations.[1] The bottom line is that only looking at humanity for direction and validation inevitably causes us to lose our way.

When we begin to live for other people (not in the healthy ways of self-sacrifice and Godly care, but in deriving our self-worth from people's acceptance), we can start to lose the proper sense of self that God desires for us. It can be like waking up inside a bad dream, wondering how we got to where we are, and not even recognizing ourselves anymore. But that's understandable since we've effectively replaced who we are and what we want for who they are and what they want. No wonder we don't recognize ourselves—we're not *us,* we're some mutated form of *them.*

When we get tired, and we lose track who we truly are to God and ourselves, it's most likely evidence that we have outpaced God in critical areas of our lives. Said another way, we've pushed ahead into territory we had no directives to enter. Whether this was trying to please someone other than him or that we started a project he never asked us to undertake, we find ourselves as the frog in the pot of boiling water.

We must recognize that God is a good father and a competent leader. This means that steady growth and proper pacing are important to him. Wherever you find the Holy Spirit, you will find health. Conversely, wherever you find lack and decay, you will be sure to find a lack of his presence.

ESSENTIAL QUESTIONS TO ask yourself include:

- Is the use of my time creating more or less health in me physically, emotionally, spiritually, and relationally?
- If I were to see my behavior in someone else, would I think they were promoting positive life decisions or negative ones?
- Is my current growth evidence of sure and steady oversight from a good Father? Or is it the reckless and chaotic route of someone driving without a license?

Our hope for you is that you would be free of living a life according to someone else's expectations for you. Instead, may you be released to live the fearless life that God wants for you as a legitimate daughter and son of the Living God.

Questioning the Call Is a Good Sign

During this crisis of calling, where we threw our hands up and told God what he could and couldn't do, we found ourselves in a unique position of wrestling with God. For those familiar with Jewish tradition, arguing with the Lord of Hosts is not a shameful thing, as we westerners might think. It's a noble thing. The story of Jacob wrestling with the angel of the Lord in Genesis 32:22–31 is seen as a praiseworthy account of a man contending with his Maker to assure a promise. God doesn't scold Jacob—if anything, he grants him the desire of his heart (and gives him a long-lasting memento of their encounter).

The point is that God is not offended by our defiant retorts. The Holy Spirit wants you to question his call for you—to wrestle it out. This means resistance, tension, and probably even some yelling. That doesn't scare God in the least, nor is it shameless or disrespectful. It's part of the path forward. Blessings always come out of wrestling with the Lord.

We don't get intimacy with God automatically, just like we don't have intimacy with people we meet randomly on the street. Intimacy with God, knowing his mind and heart, comes through trust, time, and repetition. It's also the product of collision. We don't get to deep places with God without wrestling with him—without asking tough questions and seeing things through. Unless we are willing to grapple with the Holy Spirit from time to time, we don't get far with God.

We also never get to experience any of his miracles.

God loves to prove that he is sovereign and that he can do miracles; not because he needs to reassure himself of his divinity, but because he wants to establish a meaningful relationship with us. Miracles tend to show up precisely when we need them to and not a moment before. They are one of God's many ways of saying, "I'm still here. I'm still listening. And I've got you." They also serve as reminders that we are on the right path, even when we feel tired.

When we were telling Jesus what he could and couldn't do with us in Haiti, God was not silent. Sometimes we're tempted to think that wrestling with God is a one-way fight. But the Lord Mighty in Battle is going to shove back—not more than you can handle but often more than you expected. His reply came in the form of us meeting a Haitian pastor who had used his own salary to fund 30% of a building project but had eventually run out of funds and energy.

FOR ME, James, I heard God's voice on the matter right away.

"Jamie, I can use anybody to build this church and school, including the pastor. But today, I'd like to use you. How about it?"

People often say that you can't win against God, but that's not true. You can always walk away. You can take your ball and go home. In one aspect, choosing not to play the game is its own form of victory against God. But it's certainly not a healthy way to live life, especially a Christian life. However, if we're willing to engage him, if we're ready to step into places of new obedience even when we're tired, we have the chance to see fantastic rewards.

WE DECIDED to help that pastor finish his project and fund the remaining 70% of the work. Just when we told God that we were done doing this, he sent us a project that spoke to our hearts and compelled us to want to re-engage. Today, that church has brought hundreds of people to Christ, and its school is educating hundreds of children.

If we could be so bold as to speak for the Holy Spirit in your life today, we'd like to. That's because we believe that he's speaking the same thing to you that he has been to us. "Don't underestimate how I can use you," he says. "You can't see what I can see right now. So, until you can, trust that what I'm doing in your life and where I'm leading you are far more wonderful than you can possibly imagine."

Let us echo those words: Don't underestimate how God can use you. You're not capable of seeing what he does, so basing decisions on appearances is counterproductive. Instead, discipline yourself to trust that what he says about you is accurate. This is precisely the kind of living that Paul talked about when he coined the Christian phrase "live by faith, not by sight" (2 Corinthians 5:7). Trust God with the path; he'll take care of the results.

In the next chapter, we'll discuss several action items that helped us maintain a proper perspective when walking through the more stressful parts of our journey.

TWELVE

Four Tips to Staying on Task

EVEN WHEN IT'S HARD

AS WE MENTIONED in the previous chapter, saying yes can be tremendously tricky at times (but always ridiculously rewarding). Even seemingly simple yeses can create results in unexpected challenges.

Below are four things that helped us get through periods of frustration. Like anything we offer, these may not be a perfect fit for you. But more than likely, one or two of them will help a great deal and aid you in staying true to your yeses until you get to the other side of the storms.

1.) Acknowledge Who You Are Working For

As we stood in the middle of Haiti, surrounded by poverty and overwhelmed by the magnitude of the work, we realized we were in deep need of a superior perspective. That is, we desperately needed heaven's eyes on the situation and not our own. According to human eyes, we were fighting a losing battle, and we were getting tired of people cheating one another, dragging one another through cesspools—behavioral and literal. But according to heaven, we were right where God wanted us.

Part of adopting heaven's perspective on your present circumstances comes by answering the simple question: Who do you work for? This isn't a new question by any means. Paul posed the proper answer to it when writing to the early church, saying, "Whatever you do, work at it with all your heart, as working for the Lord, not for human masters" (Colossians 3:23). In other words, even though you might be serving other people with your yeses (as all the greatest yeses are invariably about serving people), they are merely secondary characters in the story. The primary character is Jesus himself.

Serving Christ before serving others is more than just a spiritual mindset. Ultimately, it must manifest in practices that merge our time and physical resources—which includes money, property, possessions, and relationships—in ways that creatively meet the needs of others. Determining ownership is essential to obtaining heaven's perspective on your life and your work. This is also one reason why habitually giving tithes and offerings is so significant: doing so trains your mind to divest itself of owning everything it feels entitled to and, instead, recognizing that God is master of it all. We're merely stewards.

Once we realize that we are working for God and not humanity, answering the question of who our resources belong to becomes easy. Likewise, the problems you encounter aren't yours anymore—they're God's. You are merely the vessel who is trying to be faithful to what you've heard the Holy Spirit tell you. As Pastor Steven Furtick says, "Obedience is your responsibility; the outcome is God's."[1]

2.) Be a Person of Principle

When life's pressures back us into a corner, we often find out who we are. Sometimes, that person is ugly and needs a makeover. Other times, that person can surprise us and do extraordinary things.

Regardless of the person we discover when the pressure is on, you can bet that he or she is a product of what we've invested in before the crisis. This is one reason why adopting sound principles early on is critical to weathering life's storms. Godly principles, like honesty, work ethic, faithfulness to our word, and always doing our best, often help drive the car when life throws the driver in the back seat. When we don't know what to do, we often default to automatic responses. And when those responses incorporate kingdom virtues that we've taken time to cultivate beforehand, we find ourselves better equipped to handle life's unexpected turns.

But what if we haven't invested heavily in godly principles before the crisis hits? That's fine; it just means that you might find it a little harder to adopt them in the heat of the moment. Someone who has spent years applying themselves to demanding projects will have an easier time sticking with a challenge in the present versus someone who is doing it now for the first time.

Another aspect of godly ethics is that they can be taken up by anyone at any time, and they're always going to work. Since God doesn't use a "merit system," he doesn't hold our pasts against us. Instead, he looks at what we give him to work with and simply asks, "Do you want more? Because if you're willing to be faithful, I'm willing to keep providing what you need."

During our most intense seasons in Haiti, we decided to be people of principles and challenged every one of our team members to do the same. This included following through on our commitments no matter how hard it was—even when circumstances outside of our control shifted to work against us. It could have been easy to throw in the towel and play the blame game. "Well, we couldn't do what we said because of," and then fill in the blank. Instead, we found a way to make things happen and stay true to our word.

We also relied heavily upon our deep sense of personal commitment and drive. These characters traits were taught to us at an early age, and we honed them during our years in the restaurant business. Without tenacity, our restaurants wouldn't be where they are today, and we would never have had the strength to go back to Haiti after the first trip. But the extra gears under the hood allowed us to engage in ways that other people would have backed down from. It meant starting work in Haiti at 6:00 a.m. and going nonstop until 10:00 p.m. It meant letting someone's crazy accusations roll off our backs and continuing like nothing had happened. And it meant carrying on until the project was finished even if no one showed up to work. Principles always protect promises.

3.) Look for the Lessons

If we were to stop at point two above, someone might think that all meaningful kingdom-building work is tedious and life-draining. But nothing could be farther from the truth. One of our mantras is to enjoy the journey that God has us on. Without hope, without real joy in what we're doing, life is a rote exercise of pain, boredom, and insignificance. No, thank you.

Jesus proclaimed that we are called to have life, and then live it to its fullest (John 10:10). This means that we are not merely workers in a field who keep their heads down and begrudgingly endure our existence. This is the sad state of those farmers we mentioned in Drouin who can't even afford to buy their own rice. That is not the heart of God for those farmers or any of his children. There is always something in it for us—not because we are deserving in and of our own merits, but because God is a good Father.

One of the most exciting things that helps keep us motivated as people is knowing that we're learning something valuable. Sure, the process isn't always the most glamorous.

But if you think back in your life to some of the most meaningful seasons, we bet you those were somehow connected with valuable lessons. Whether in school or life, learning and growth go hand in hand with a sense of true fulfillment. Knowing that God is teaching us something through what we're going through can sustain us in surprising ways.

Even though 2017 was a challenging year for us in Haiti, we knew God was leading us forward—teaching us, and adding rich experiences to our lives that we couldn't purchase any other way. That sense of "the new" and "the unknown" kept us coming back even when our flesh was tired and we had bad attitudes. And God will do the same for you, but only if you are willing to recognize the value of his mentorship in your life.

4.) Mentor Up, Reach Out

We've already discussed the importance of strategic relationships, but it's worth emphasizing again. We are only as rich as the lives of those people we've allowed into our head- and heart-space. Recognizing areas of your life that are weak and then asking God to fill in the cracks with other strong people is not a sign of weakness; it's a sign of immense strength and wisdom.

As we mentioned before, Mike Shipman taught us new ways of dealing with spiritual needs, while Kirk Gilchrist challenged us to think more broadly about our call to business *and* ministry. Reaching out to form new, mutually beneficial partnerships opens doors of favor that are immeasurably important to your work, both now and in the future. Treat those relationships with great care. Nurture them with an occasional call, text, or email when the thought hits you, even if you're not working with that person in the moment. You'll be surprised to learn how little effort is required to keep that relationship alive until the moment where one or both of you needs the other person's unique abilities for a kingdom-minded project.

Finding mentors in your life is equally important. For us, John Maxwell has been a resource of immense wisdom and perspective. There is no way we can live a life that exactly mirrors his. Nor can we accelerate time and become as old as he is (years being a commodity we treasure, not despise). So to have access to his caliber of insights, to be in proximity to him as a person, is an honor we couldn't buy with all the money in the world. When an older-wiser chooses to take you under their wing, it is a gift. If you seek mentorship humbly and pursue it faithfully, it will help sustain you when everything else seems lost.

AS YOU CONFRONT the storms that saying yes invariably brings, remember that you are not alone—that God intends for you to partner with other people to get the job done. Look for the valuable, exciting, and unique lessons that the Holy Spirit is gifting to you (he's the *best* teacher too). Stick to the principles that got you this far; they'll help you finish what you started. And lastly, remember who it is that you're working for. While you might be surrounded by humans—ones who tend to get us off course—it is ultimately God who you are serving. As Paul wrote, "find out what pleases the Lord," and then be sure to do it (Ephesians 5:10).

THIRTEEN

Taking on the Impossible

"YOU WANT US TO WHAT?"

I, James, was beside myself as I sat across from a European businessman who had invited me to dinner under what some might say were false pretenses. He wasn't malicious about it—far from! And in my heart, I knew what he was asking was yet another yes opportunity from God. I just hadn't expected the question.

It was August of 2018, and Sarah and I were looking into the possibility of building a Burger King in Toussaint Louverture International Airport in Port-au-Prince. We wanted to see if we could create an indigenous business that didn't rely on constant monies from the United States but, instead, generated revenue in-country that could be used to fund feeding children, and building schools and churches. Haitians feeding Haitians was becoming our dream, and leveraging our experience with Burger King and Haiti's existing business community seemed a logical next step.

To that end, Sarah and I did our homework. Not only did we get the go-ahead from corporate and from the airport, but we dug into the legal, demographic, economic, and political issues surrounding the possible venture. More importantly, we had proven something essential to the community: that they, the Haitian people, could take care of themselves. It was only a matter of time before the foreigners got out of the way.

In the process of our research, a contact introduced us to a well-connected, well-respected European entrepreneur named Damien. We were not only excited to have his access to the airport and Haiti's Minister of Finance, but to Damien himself, who was deeply invested in the people. After my five-hour drive to the ferry-accessible island of Ile a Vache and our hours-long dinner at Damien's home where he'd invited me to discuss the details of building a Burger King, I was floored when he suddenly shifted gears.

"I want to talk about something else," he said.

"Sure," I replied. "What's on your mind?"

"Can you come to my island and feed my children?"

I stared at Damien dumbstruck. *Aren't we here to discuss indigenous business models?* I thought. I was in shock, and certainly not prepared to answer that question.

Or was I?

"Yes, of course we will," I replied, and then realized I had spoken without thinking.

Because yeses compound by nature, it shouldn't come as

Living a Life of Yes

any surprise when new and more profound yes opportunities present themselves. Said another way, building a track record of saying yes to God invites him to open unimaginable doors. Like the scriptures say, he "is able to do immeasurably more than all we ask or imagine, according to his power that is at work within us" (Ephesians 3:20). And what is that power at work inside of us? It is the power that enabled Jesus to say yes to the Father's invitation to the cross in Luke 22:42, where he just pushed aside what his flesh wanted and embraced what his Father wanted—"not my will, but yours."

I had no idea at the time, but I had just committed Elevating Christian Ministries to feeding 5,000 children on Ile a Vache across thirty secular schools with no public transportation. I mention that these were "secular" schools on purpose, in that all schools on the mainland were Christian-run. As a result, this opportunity was not only our most sizable venture to date, but it was also the first time we were being invited into the non-church community to serve children. We, as the church, were going to be doing what the government was unable to.

But the yes opportunity came with several sobering mountains to climb. As always, the greater the chance, the higher the stakes. We were about to double the number of children we were feeding in Haiti, and we would be doing so on a remote island for twice the cost of standard transportation of goods and labor. And—oh yeah—there was no electricity.

You can probably imagine how I felt as I left that meeting. If you guessed overwhelmed and in way over my head, you guessed right. *You just said yes, Jamie,* I thought to myself. *Nice job. Now you've got to pull this off.*

What was I thinking?

But God knew what he was doing. He was the one who led me to Damien's house. Likewise, he was the one who'd opened the doors for us to work in Haiti for the last eighteen months. And all those years of building businesses, developing teams, and learning how to manage wealth were part of God's divine genius. He is the master builder; we are just the workers.

Wherever you are at today, know that God is inviting you to step into the next thing if you will be faithful to and enjoy the process of the current thing. This doesn't mean that you love all aspects of your current situation: some things do genuinely suck. But the Holy Spirit's presence in the midst of your challenges?—that never sucks. His presence is a gift, and one we would be wise not to scorn.

That night, I called up Sarah to explain what I had committed us to. "Do you have any idea how big this is?"

She replied, "Do you have any idea how big our God is?"

Point: Sarah.

We laughed and realized we were, once again, enjoying the favor of God in the midst of feeling like we were living on life's edge. And the truth is, there's no better place to be. Remember, so much of what people think of as "comfortable living" is actually a life of saying no. The best, most vibrant, most fulfilling life we can lead is one where we embrace God's ideas for us and leap into his arms.

When Heaven Gets Behind You

As we looked into feeding the children of Ile a Vache, something profound began to happen. The opportunity's once impassable mountainous terrain started to flatten out. We began to come up with solutions to circumstances that, moments before, seemed impossible. The more we sought God, pressed into the work to the exclusion of all other distractions, and thought about the needs of those children, the more ideas seemed to present themselves as if out of thin air.

It's only when we are pressed that we begin to access previously unknown realms of heaven. Bible verses that were once mere ink on pages or text on screens suddenly take on new meaning. "In all your ways submit to him, and he will make your paths straight" (Proverbs 3:6). Yahweh spoke through the Old Testament prophet and said, "I am making a way in the wilderness and streams in the wasteland," and again, "I will go before you and will level the mountains" (Isaiah 43:19; 45:2). And God's promise to Israel resonates with us to this day when he said, "Be strong and courageous. Do not be afraid or terrified because of them, for the Lord your God goes with you; he will never leave you nor forsake you" (Deuteronomy 31:6). What was fear became faith as we looked through the eyes of possibility.

As ideas unfolded and turned into action, we felt as if all our previous experiences were leading us to yet another Esther Moment. The Old Testament story tells of a beautiful woman who took an unlikely route to become queen. Once there, she was faced with the choice of saving her own life or sparing her people. But the decision was made easier when her uncle pointed out that her entire life up until that point had been preparation, such that he proposed, "And who knows but that you have come to your royal position for such a time as this?" (Esther 4:14).

Your life has been the staging ground for your next yes opportunity. Whether it's big or small when compared to what other people are going through is irrelevant. What matters is what your current yes means to you and your relationship with God. As we discussed before, finding the joy of God's favor is critical to your efforts. While Jesus was faced with the most painful death ever invented by humanity, Roman crucifixion, the writer of Hebrews noted: "For the joy set before him he endured the cross" (Hebrews 12:2b). Meaning, there is something beautiful to be found when we're faced with the impossible. We won't discover it, however, by keeping our eyes on our circumstances; it's only when we choose to look toward the Holy Spirit for help that we find out the joy of tackling our next big yes and taking its challenges head-on.

Progress Is Progressional

By the next month, ECM had built one bakery that was serving six schools and 1,000 children. It was our prototype. We realized we could not take on all 5,000 children at once as we needed to develop and test systems. Overcoming the island's inherent obstacles was a logistical nightmare, but we worked it until we had viable solutions. We knew we could expand by employing multiple bakeries around a central baking center and then using motorcycles to serve every school on the island. It wasn't going to be easy, but with the Holy Spirit's help, it was going to get done.

One of the potential pitfalls of living a life of yes is jumping into the "doing" too quickly, rather than exploring the "being." Many people get into trouble when they say yes and confuse that with thinking they have all the pieces figured out, or that everything will just magically happen for them. While there is undoubtedly much to be said for divine intervention, as our lives have shown, there is much more to be said for God insisting that we, his children made in his image, do due diligence with every opportunity he gifts to us.

Learning to sit with the prospects, investigate the possibilities, and develop healthy systems is as much a part of saying yes as is the completion of a project. Remember, there is a difference between saying yes and executing a yes well. We didn't want to feed the children of Ile a Vache once and be done; we wanted to put systems in place that would last long after we were gone. Again, we wanted Haitians feeding Haitians, so we let them take over the model. If it wasn't going to be a Burger King, then it was going to be something else. Our job was to remain flexible and work hard with the tools and resources Jesus had given us.

An interesting thing about prototypes besides proving a concept is that they tend to attract investors—at least good prototypes do. Within two months, right when we were looking to expand operations into 2019, our senior pastor, Pierre du Plessis, informed us that our church, The Father's House, wanted to help fund the feeding of children on Ile e Vache. Just like that, the church's $30,000 contribution allowed us to expand operations and feed all 5,000 children for six months.

The fact is, for all our planning and hard work, there was one thing we couldn't account for in our equations: God's hand. And neither can you. What's truly amazing about this concept of mixing faith and facts is that God invites us into the story with only half the picture. And he does so on purpose. "Why would a loving God ever do something so manipulative?" critics may ask. But it's not manipulative. It's playful. God loves to collaborate with us, which means he has stuff to bring to the table just like we do. Faith means having patience enough to wait on God while we're engaged with our own aspect of the equation. Then, when we do see God come behind it, the feeling is ridiculous. We know with everything we are that we can't create the impossible—only he can do that. And then we are reminded, once again, that there's no way that we can fulfill a yes without God.

FOURTEEN

Living on the Other Side of Yes

MANAGING EXPONENTIAL GROWTH

BY LATE 2019, ECM was feeding 8,500 children over 1-million rolls over a forty-week school year. As of the writing of this book in 2020, those figures have climbed to over 30,000 children and 2.4-million rolls. And we expect the statistics to keep climbing as we set our sights on feeding 35,000 children per day. We're also exploring new business ventures, including construction companies, cement block manufacturing, jewelry design and production, and even livestock breeding of chickens, goats, and cows. There is more opportunity now than ever before.

Seeing these results inspires us, just as we hope they inspire you. But it's imperative to remember that none of this happened overnight, and neither will your fruitfulness. Learning to say yes takes time, and it requires an extraordinary level of diligence to pursue. Likewise, managing growth is not an accident and requires that we build upon the foundations that got us to where we are.

Here are six tips we employ when managing all the various activities God has allowed us to be a part of. If we hadn't learned these tips, you would probably not be reading this book—at least not from us.

1.) Keep Recording, Keep Talking

As one yes leads to another, one success leads to another. Mind you, we don't subscribe to the notion that all success is of the financial sort—more on that in a moment. But being able to measure things that we invest in has its benefits, and God certainly isn't ashamed of numbers—he sure did a lot of calculating with Israel in the book of Numbers.

Keeping track of your life is not only an excellent way to let those coming after you know what you did, but it serves as a valuable tool for recounting what God has done in and through you. Whatever your methods may be, we encourage you to at least keep an annual accounting of what the Lord has done in your life. This book wouldn't have been written without the practice of remembering and writing down what God has done for us.

Part of keeping an account also means talking about what Jesus is doing in you and through you. Recounting miracle stories not only creates faith in others but builds even more faith in you. Be quick to share what God is doing and slow to entertain what God is not. In our minds, we do the easy stuff; God does the hard stuff. We answer the call, but God makes the connections.

There is a beautiful section of God's instructions to the children of Israel in the Old Testament book of Deuteronomy that speaks to the importance of remembrance in the life of believers.

> *18 Fix these words of mine in your hearts and minds; tie them as symbols on your hands and bind them on your foreheads. 19 Teach them to your children, talking about them when you sit at home and when you walk along the road, when you lie down and when you get up. 20 Write them on the doorframes of your houses and on your gates, 21 so that your days and the days of your children may be many in the land the Lord swore to give your ancestors, as many as the days that the heavens are above the earth.*
> —Deuteronomy 11

One of the many advantages of keeping recordings is being able to evaluate what new opportunities line up with what you're naturally gifted at. Themes begin to emerge that help us identify profitable and, therefore, worthwhile ventures. Those themes help us identify seemingly promising opportunities that, because they lay outside of our giftedness, are most likely distractions.

Writing down memories and tracking God's blessings helps reveal where we have been and point to where we are heading. Slow down, pay attention to the details, and enjoy the moments you are in because life happens in real-time. When we slow down and pay attention, we accomplish far more than by running twice as fast.

2.) Value People Above Profits

While this may sound easy, it's often harder than most people realize. Until you're faced with the dilemma of losing money or losing people, you will never really know the moral, ethical, and emotional challenges of such a predicament.

One of the best ways to stay clear of harming people, inadvertently or intentionally, is remembering that people don't follow a vision first, they follow you. Children don't model their parents because they subscribe to adult ideology; they mimic behavior because of proximity. As another example, Christians follow Jesus because of who he is, not because of his vision for the world—that's merely a benefit. Jesus didn't give his disciples some grand look at past, present, and future and then ask for their allegiance. Instead, he spoke to young fishermen and simply said, "Follow me." Once again, people follow people before they follow ideas.

If we create a habit of only following people because of what they can do for us and not because of who they are to us, we set ourselves up for disappointments. The result is a life of bitterness and resentment. Instead, our mission is to build meaningful relationships. Some end up becoming valuable ministry and business partnerships, but not all. That's because productivity isn't the point—being present for one another is.

For the first twenty years of our professional lives, we were self-centered. Our most significant shift was when we started putting others before ourselves and recognized that there is a difference between care and value.

If we value that an employee showed up for work but do not care that they had a horrible day at home, we are putting profits above people. When we move beyond value and into the realm of care, we become concerned about an employee's battle with depression over not being able to afford reliable transportation. So, when we can, we buy them a car.

One of our managers' daughters needed eye surgery that wasn't covered by insurance, so we paid for it. We got involved beyond the cash register.

Another of our managers was unable to fly home to Puerto Rico because of extenuating circumstances. So we purchased tickets for her parents to come to see her in New York. It was the first time in ten years she'd seen her family. But then she made an astounding statement: "I feel like I have more of a family with you than I do in Puerto Rico."

Just last week, amid the most significant economic depression the United States has seen since the 1930s, we heard of a pastor in dire need of a vehicle, so we purchased him a car.

Some of you reading this can't just go off and buy cars for people, while others of you can afford to buy fifty vehicles. Whatever your circumstances, we must remember that our lives can't just be words, they must be actions. Serving our employees isn't only professional, it's personal. As we said before, money is not what impresses people the most: your time does. If you take care of your people, whether in business, ministry, or family life, profits will come. Business and ministry have this in common: they are always built on the pillar of putting other people first.

3.) ROI vs. ROI

There are two different ROI acronyms for the life of a Christian. The first is the one that every good investor knows: return on investment. This encompasses what an investor gets back in the way of financial dividends. The second, reward of investment, is native to the kingdom of heaven, and it has to do with many of the spiritual intangibles we can't easily quantify. Since God's economy is dependent solely upon him and does not expand or contract according to fickle markets or human strategies, returns on investment are irrelevant here, but rewards of investing are everything.

Unlike monetary returns, which can be calculated and quantified, rewards are often intangible and only realized later—some not at all. A reward is typically given in recognition of service and, very often, has no monetary value attached to it. Instead, it carries the weight of a nominating body or an entire populace. In God's Kingdom, rewards come with his pleasure—the most fabulous prize of all—and that can never be fully seen until we are with him in glory. While we may not see immediate results for things that cost us, nothing is ever wasted in God's kingdom.

As of the writing of this book, we are living in a whirlwind because of all the things that we're saying yes to. And unlike some who may fear the flurry of activity, we thrive on it because we long to be in the center of what God is doing, not on the fringes. That is not to say that busyness equates to godliness, but having your hearts, resources, and actions aligned with his plans certainly does.

The exciting thing about this kind of living and giving is the compounding factor that exists in God's kingdom. Sowing seeds is an activity where faith sees the harvest. One yes begets the next, and those yeses have ways of multiplying exponentially. We would never have fathomed the checks that we're writing today, some of which are our salary seven years ago going into kingdom-building enterprises.

Non-financial rewards mean that lives are still being changed. There is no financial blessing for bringing water to a village. Likewise, we have no ledgers on the financial returns of feeding children. To an accountant, these activities are categorized as "financial losses." But it's the lives that are being impacted that matters, most of which we'll never know about.

It's not our job to know if the kingdom is going to be fruitful. That's God's job. We would rather go bankrupt for the kingdom than make any money on the earth. Keep sowing and resist the tendency to worry about the outcomes. Sowing is hard work that we mustn't be afraid of; may your prayer be like ours: "God, if someone needs to do it, please let it be me."

Resist the urge to get shortsighted, throw up your hands and ask, "What's the point?" God's work is eternal, and some things we won't have answers for until we're in eternity with him. That's not a cop-out, that's simply a reality of the Christian experience. Learn to recognize that the Holy Spirit is with you, and his presence is enough.

Remember, there is a difference between return on investment and reward of investment. One yields short-term consequences, and the other has eternal significance. Choose wisely.

4.) The Power of the Proper People

Similar to the above, surround yourself with others who believe in you and your vision. Some strategic relationships are cultivated intentionally, while others appear to be accidental. But both are necessary. Our job is to be aware of the most important people in our lives and seek to nurture those relationships.

One of the many benefits of investing in genuine relationships is that those people can help weed out the wrong yeses. This underlines the importance of being careful of who you spend time around. Wise counsel can help determine what is from God and what is not. Aren't convinced? The "wisest man who ever lived," King Solomon, surely thought so, as he spoke to the matter three times in scripture (Proverbs 11:14; 15:22; and 24:6).

Surround yourself with people who believe in your significance. Their wisdom and encouragement water the seeds of your next yes.

If you're reading this and thinking, "That's awesome. But how do I find such high-caliber people?" The long answer probably deserves another book. The short answer, however, is to ask for them.

There is a powerful verse in James that says, "you do not have because you do not ask God" (James 4:2). This is potentially derived from Jesus's words in the Gospel of Matthew, where he says, "Ask and it will be given to you; seek and you will find; knock and the door will be opened to you. For everyone who asks receives; the one who seeks finds; and to the one who knocks, the door will be opened" (Matthew 7:7–8).

When our businesses were becoming successful and we started attending church again, we recognized that God had given us hands and feet, sharp minds, and good work ethics. But even in light of all our abilities, we were simply unable to do everything ourselves. What we lacked were good friendships.

At that time, we believed that it was selfish to ask God for something for ourselves. But the more time we spent reading and studying God's word, the more we realized that it was Godly to ask him for what we did not have as it forced us to recognize Jesus as our ultimate provider.

So, we started asking for friends. Granted, at that time in our lives, we had none. We're not even sure we could say we were friends with our employees. But we recognized the need for friends, confidants, and mentors, and we put the weight on God to help us do what we could not.

The same week we quietly started asking the Holy Spirit for friends, our pastors invited us over for dinner and introduced us to several individuals who remain our friends to this day. God brought us people that would have never connected with us otherwise, all because we asked. And not only that, but the Holy Spirit continues to bring us new friends, ones we believe are a direct result of our original prayer.

5.) Faith Over Fear

As we've discussed previously, people often allow fear to dictate their response to opportunity. Few things can snuff out hope as quickly fear can. Many of us are terrified to make the first move needed to step out for a yes invitation, while others find themselves too far into a project to back out but not far enough to see the end, so we seize up. Either way, fear can be crippling.

But lingering in the heart of every Christian is a spark that, when blown upon by the breath of the Holy Spirit, wants to burn brightly for his purposes. Whatever your means of overcoming fear may be, from therapy and counseling to reminding yourself of times where you stepped out in faith in the past, fight for your freedom from fear. And you have good reason to be encouraged in your battle: Jesus himself is rooting for you (Hebrews 7:25; Romans 8:34).

Bravery is trying something despite being afraid. But

bravery can be exhausting if fear of the unknown doesn't eventually transform into some measure of trust in God. Being perpetually afraid of failure is debilitating and is no way to live life. Many people want to get close to God; they just don't want to rely on him, especially when he says, "Jump!"

Resolve to be someone who attempts something, embraces failure as a possible result, and decides in advance to grow from the outcome. If growth is the goal, then every route will afford some measure of success. In the words of the famed father of modern missions, William Carey, "Expect great things from God; attempt great things for God."[1] By saying yes, you close the door on fear, and you kick it in the teeth. Your new yeses will sow seeds that determine the harvest of your future.

Our first steps into yes invitations can often be hard, we know. But once we accept our unique chance to be the first person to say yes, God has a unique way of meeting us on the threshold of faith. Put things on the line, and make it cost you something, and then watch what God will do with your offering.

But that's not even the coolest part.

If you say yes, others will too. And then you have the unique opportunity to speak to their fears and doubts from the place of seeing God come through for you.

Additionally, look for opportunities to push your faith a little further. It's not tomorrow's step you have to consider, it's today's. Resist the pull toward ease and comfort. Instead, sit on the edge of your seat and look to anticipate what the Holy

Spirit might be up to next. Not only is this fun, but it signals to heaven that you're ready for more.

The more we get, the more we want to give it all away. All this may sound like a "one blessing after the other" mantra, and in a sense, that's true. But at the core of it all is a deep, desperate desire to please God and see the dreams of his heart come true.

At the end of a person's life, one of their greatest sorrows will not be the measure of pain they experienced—pain is universal. It will be how many things they missed because they refused to say yes—that is true sadness. Conversely, joy is living life in such a way that we can look back on all the opportunities the Holy Spirit brought to us and say, "I said yes to that one, and that one, and that one," and spend our final breaths recounting his goodness.

6.) Pitch a Wide Tent, Cast a Wide Net

A theme in the Old Testament is that of extending one's tent. Explicitly, the prophet Isaiah declares to Yahweh in poetic verse, if not song, "Enlarge the place of your tent, stretch your tent curtains wide, do not hold back" (Isaiah 54:2). While this metaphor is mostly lost on us today, it can regain much of its power if we were to say to a friend, "I'm praying you get a bigger house." The inference, of course, is that a bigger house can hold more people and more possessions. But a bigger house also requires more wealth in order to manage the property, utilities, and maintenance. It is, for all intents and purposes, saying, "I hope you become hugely successful."

The point of the scripture, as is our point here, was not to imply the desire of wealth for wealth's sake, but rather to help fulfill the Abrahamic covenant that we are blessed to be a blessing (Genesis 12:2–3). Said more simply, don't be afraid to let others enjoy your blessings.

Our friend Sammy was not raised in a Christian home and, as such, had never donated money or possessions in her whole life. But we wanted to share the blessings of our work in Haiti with her, so we invited her on a trip. The intent was not to get her to give or transform her life, even though we suspected such things might happen. Instead, we felt the trip would touch her profoundly and enrich the already fantastic person that she was. Sammy hadn't been in-country more than a few hours before she felt compelled to be a part of the work we were doing, and she gave financially for the first time in her life.

An estranged classmate of Jamie's, a man we'll call Will, lost his home in a house fire, and soon after his son got into a severe car accident. We were able to lend Will one of our homes until he got back on his feet. As a result, the fractured friendship was miraculously healed, and Will was able to provide for his family.

While at a restaurant once, a bartender overheard part of Sarah's testimony and was deeply touched, and she expressed a sincere interest in Jesus. Something as significant as a tableside conversation can have dramatic effects in the hands of the Holy Spirit.

The point is that we can never know the significance of our conversations, and we never know who is watching. Even the most horrible things can be turned around when we are willing to let the blessings of our lives—monetary or otherwise—become influencing agents in God's hands. So dramatic was the restoration of the relationship with Will that Jamie even said, "I'm so glad your house burned down," and Will agreed. God's economy is often hard to figure out, but we can never argue with the results.

Similar to the Old Testament theme of pitching a wide tent is a New Testament idea of casting a wide net (Matthew 4:12-23, John 21:1-6). Unlike the expansion of the home in the previous texts, Jesus instructed his disciples to employ different fishing methods in order to catch more fish. Here, the emphasis is on increasing what we are going after rather than what we are housing.

As is often our habit in our northern home city of Rochester, New York, we gave out hundreds of free cheeseburgers at Christmas. This particular year, we wanted to up the Christmas spirit and gave out bikes to children too. Several of the kids who received cheeseburgers and bikes couldn't figure out why we were giving them things. To our dismay, we discovered that they didn't even know it was Christmas.

Your willingness to give from your place of blessing has the potential to transform someone's entire life paradigm.

Living a Life of Yes

Your Future Is Waiting

There is nothing more fulfilling than living from the abundance of your purpose. Every day, each of us is faced with choices to either engage God in the matters of our future or recede into the shadows of our past. Sure, any one of us could just "keep doing what we're doing" and watch life slip by. But we don't believe anyone is meant for that kind of life, least of all you.

Life becomes exciting when we replace the question, "What am I going to do for myself today?" with, "God, what would you like me to do today?" If we pray this prayer enough, and then collaborate with the Holy Spirit when he shows up to answer it, living for Christ becomes a lifestyle, not a wish.

Living on the other side of yes takes faith. Like a surfer who paddles hard to crest the wave, it can be a struggle to climb out of a trough. But once you're on the other side, the momentum seems to be perpetual—a limitless ride powered by nothing less than the majesty of the ocean itself. Many people describe this as a breaking point between how they used to live and to how they're living today. It's a mindset change, one made through habitual and sometimes dogmatic determination to put God first.

Saying yes is expensive.

Saying yes can invite spiritual resistance.

Saying yes will force us to confront our shortcomings and selfishness, and it will put us in the middle of other people's messes.

But saying yes is also the greatest act of obedience we can offer God, one that he is faithful to reward. Effort is essential, but not impressive; only obedience is remarkable.

Today, you have a choice to live out of your purpose or just keep doing what you're doing. Our prayer is that you choose to use all your energy in pursuing your purpose, walking in his pleasure, and looking toward heaven to say, "Okay, God. What's next?"

Learn More

For more information on our work in Haiti and how you can be a part, visit **elevating.org** today.

Endnotes

1. Kill the Common Life

1. Rob Picheta, "The World is Sadder and Angrier Than Ever, Major Study Finds," *CNN*, April 25, 2019, https://www.cnn.com/2019/04/25/health/gallup-world-emotions-index-scli-intl/index.html (accessed March 2020); cf. "Gallup 2019 Global Emotions Report," *Gallup*, April 25, 2019, https://www.gallup.com/analytics/248906/gallup-global-emotions-report-2019.aspx (accessed March 2020).

5. Is This Happening?

1. Lynne Warberg, as quoted by Sharon Guynup, "Haiti: Possessed by Voodoo," *National Geographic*, July 7, 2004, https://www.nationalgeographic.com/news/2004/7/haiti-ancient-traditions-voodoo/close (accessed March 2020).
2. The World Bank, "The World Bank in Haiti: Overview," https://www.worldbank.org/en/country/haiti/overview (accessed March 2020).

6. Breaking for Haiti

1. US Central Intelligence Agency, "The World Factbook: Haiti," https://www.cia.gov/library/publications/the-world-factbook/geos/ha.html (accessed March 2020). Cf. Center for Poverty Research, University of California, Davis, "What is the current poverty rate in the United States?" https://poverty.ucdavis.edu/faq/what-current-poverty-rate-united-states (accessed March 2020).

7. There's No Such Thing as a Bad Yes

1. Paul E. Billheimer, *Don't Waste Your Sorrows: New Insight Into God's Eternal Purpose for Each Christian in the Midst of Life's Greatest Adversities* (Fort Washington, Pennsylvania: CLC Publications, June 1977).

8. Building Greatness Out of Yeses

1. Maura R. O'Connor, "Subsidizing Starvation: How American tax dollars are keeping Arkansas rice growers fat on the farm and starving millions of Haitians," https://foreignpolicy.com/2013/01/11/subsidizing-starvation/ (accessed March 2020).
2. Bill Clinton, Democracy Now, "'We Made a Devil's Bargain': Fmr. President Clinton Apologizes for Trade Policies that Destroyed Haitian Rice Farming," https://www.democracynow.org/2010/4/1/clinton_rice (accessed March 2020); BBC News, "US urged to stop Haiti rice subsidies," https://www.bbc.com/news/world-latin-america-11472874 (accessed March 2020).

10. Empowering Others to Discover Their Yeses

1. Steve Corbett and Brian Fikkert, *When Helping Hurts: Alleviating Poverty Without Hurting the Poor... and Yourself* (Chicago: Moody Publishers, June 2009).
2. Robert D. Lupton, Toxic Charity: How the Church Hurts Those They Help and How to Reverse It (New York: Harper Collins, October 2011).
3. J. Gregory Dees, "A Tale of Two Cultures: Charity, Problem Solving, and the Future of Social Entrepreneurship," *Journal of Business Ethics*, volume 111, August 17, 2012, https://link.springer.com/article/10.1007%2Fs10551-012-1412-5 (accessed March 2020).

11. When Yes Feels Too Heavy

1. Melody Beattie, *Codependent No More: How to Stop Controlling Others and Start Caring for Yourself* (Center City, MN: Hazelden Publishing, 1986); Henry Cloud and John Townsend, *Boundaries: When to Say Yes, How to Say No to Take Control of Your Life* (Grand Rapids: Zondervan, January 1992).

12. Four Tips to Staying on Task

1. Steven Furtick, Twitter, https://twitter.com/stevenfurtick/status/920390231198785536, October 17, 2017 (accessed March 2020).

14. Living on the Other Side of Yes

1. William Carey, *The Baptist Herald and Friend of Africa* (October 1842), and "The Missionary Herald" in *The Baptist Magazine*, Vol. 35 (January 1843), p. 41.

Made in the USA
Middletown, DE
25 February 2021